Joe McGee was born in Hartford, Connecticut. He has been involved in the technical industry since the year 2000. He has been involved in speaking topics such as: *"Building Team Dynamics"* and *"Leadership Lessons Inspired by a 6-year-old"*; which have been expanded into the topics in this book.

Joe McGee presently works for Konica Minolta as a Call Center Manager. He lives in Connecticut with his wife, Amanda, and his three children: Ursula, Nathan, and Tabitha.

About The Illustrator/Artist
Philip Danse

Mr. Philip Danse has a BA in art. He lives in Keystone Heights, Florida, with his wife, Bette. Mr. Danse has had a lifelong interest in ancient civilizations and symbols, and incorporates them in many of his paintings. His favorite art mediums are acrylics and charcoal.

For more information about Philip Danse' work, please visit his Art Gallery at: *http://www.my-art-gems.com/art24bio.htm*

About The Editor
Mia Darien

Born a Connecticut Yankee in nobody's court, Mia Darien grew up to brave snow and talk fast. She started reading when she was three and never looked back. She soon started frequently falling asleep with a book under her cheek (something she still does. Although these days, it's her Nook as often as a paperback).

At eleven, she discovered *Night Mare* by Piers Anthony and entered the world of grown-up fantasy fiction and it all started from there. She started writing at fourteen, then met vampires as a teenager; and the concept for what would become *Adelheid* was soon born. Epic fantasy remains her first love, but she enjoys writing whatever stories come to mind, in any genre.

Now, she loves both writing and helping her indie community with her freelancing. A geek till the end, she enjoys role-play by e-mail games and *World of Warcraft* when she has the time. Married to her very own 'Named Man of the North,' she lives with him, their mini-tank (also known as their son) and pets, who usually act more childish than the child.

More information about Mia Darien can be found on her website at: *http://miadarien.com*.

Dedication

This book is dedicated to my daughter, Ursula Morgana McGee, whose mind continues to grow with curiosity.

Ursula Morgana McGee, 6 years old.

"You can't tell me" – Ursula McGee

Joseph McGee

LEADERSHIP LESSONS INSPIRED BY A 6 YEAR OLD

AUSTIN MACAULEY PUBLISHERS[tm]

London • Cambridge • New York • Sharjah

Ordering Information:
Quantity sales: special discounts are available on quantity purchases by corporations, associations, and others. For details, contact the publisher at the address below.

Publishers cataloging in publishing data
McGee, Joseph.
Leadership Lessons Inspired By a 6 Year Old

ISBN 9781641820967 (Paperback)
ISBN 9781641820950 (Hardback)
ISBN 9781641820974 (E-Book)

The main category of the book — Business & Economics / Management Science

www.austinmacauley.com

First Published (2018)
Austin Macauley Publishers Ltd™
40 Wall Street, 28th Floor
New York, NY 10005
USA

mail-usa@austinmacauley.com
+1 (646) 5125767

Acknowledgment

Thank you to the following individuals. Without their contributions and support, this book would not have been written:

Amanda McGee – Wife
Nathan McGee & Tabitha McGee – Son and Daughter
Patrick McGee – Orgone Energy
Ursula McGee – Daughter and Inspiration for this book
Heath Hunt – Mentor and Friend

Illustrator: Philip Danse
Editor: Mia Darien

Table of Content

Preface

In leadership, there is no operating manual for how to manage a team. It's through experiences you find your way through the journey of leadership.

I first stepped into the technical support industry in the year 2000. Over the course of time, I've had many roles such as being a website developer, sales manager, technical support analyst, trainer. These eventually led me to a leadership role. Earlier in my career, it was evident that I would continue to have a technical role. My favorite role was training people, and the ability to teach others. By doing so, my favorite part was to see the progression and difference I made in their life. For me, the biggest payoff was for others to see that I had more potential in what I was capable of. When you take it upon yourself to take on more, is when success will find you.

Leadership started for me in 2009, when I emerged from being a technical support analyst and accepted a leadership role. Any new leader knows it can be scary going from an individual contributor to a leader.

During the same year, I was blessed with the birth of my daughter, Ursula McGee in August. One may not at first relate fatherhood and leadership in the same sentence, but I have learned first-hand that a relationship exists.

As time moved forward and years passed, many lessons and questions have come from my daughter. In raising her, I've seen that the transparencies of raising a daughter and molding a team are very similar.

I'm proud to share these leadership lessons that have helped shape me as a leader by raising my daughter and using the same lessons in the workplace. Step into my shoes and learn new ways and techniques as a manager, to develop and challenge your team. These experiences are based on call center environments, but the principles throughout the book can apply to any environment.

Whether you are new to leadership or looking for new ways to shape your team, this book will leave you with many things that can spark creativity. I hope you enjoy this book and are ready to make some changes that will influence a more productive work force. This is my journey...

1. Stop Blurred Vision

How many of us have a drawer—or perhaps a shoebox of pictures? Maybe pictures didn't make the cut and are tucked away from the eyes of others. But for what reason? One might say these pictures are not considered 'perfect.' The pictures defined as 'perfect' are hanging neatly on the wall of our homes, to treasure that 'perfect moment.' What is the definition of a good or bad picture? Don't be so quick to judge. What are your first thoughts of the picture below? Would you hang this picture in your house?

Family Picture: Left to Right (Ursula, Tabitha, Amanda, Nathan and I.)

This photo was taken in 95 degrees Fahrenheit weather at Disney's Magic Kingdom in July of 2015.

My daughter noticed that I had this picture as my PC wallpaper. She said, "Daddy, that's a bad picture."

I said, "Why is it a bad picture?"

My daughter said, "Nobody is looking, and look at Tabbi's hand."

I said to her, "No. This is a great picture, because it tells a story." Let's study the picture and you will see it does in fact, tell a story. During this sweltering day, my daughter is distracted by a parade nearby in the far corner.

"Do you remember the parade when we first got to the park?" I asked my daughter.

My daughter then realized and said, "Don't be so quick to judge."

This picture is much more than just something we tuck aside and put away. It tells a story. I challenge you to wipe the dust off those old pictures and hang them up, or share them and ignite stories that could be used for enjoyable conversation pieces.

Perfection should be your own definition and not what everyone else thinks 'perfect' is.

As an example, if I conducted a social experiment in which—let's say, we were at a doctor's office and every 15 minutes a buzzer went off. During this experiment, everyone is in on it, expect one person. When the buzzer goes off, everyone stands up and then sits back down. Do you think you would follow their lead, not knowing why they are doing it? I bet you would.

We must not follow and make our own decisions and definitions in life.

Well, "how does this apply to leadership?" you might ask. One of the biggest mistakes that leaders make is: judging by facts before hearing the other side's story. One of the things we must do as leaders is: judge based on facts, until you listen and understand things in other's shoes. We need to look beyond the texture of the problem and not jump to conclusions. It's an unwise decision until we ask questions.

For example, let's say you found a recording of your direct report saying something not in scope of policy. Before telling them, "This is what I saw," and coming up with a plan so that it does not happen again, you acted too quickly. And then nobody learns. The best course of action is listening to their side first. Tell them what you have and ask questions; find out their reason and reaction first.

For example, if I heard the agent speak with a condescending tone or imitating a race – I want the agent to realize this themselves. Have the agent listen to the call and ensure they understand what you have uncovered. If you as the manager just tell them what you have then who is really learning? The answer is nobody.

Don't be so quick to judge. Much like the example of the picture, we answered questions, explained the situation, and listened to why it was a good picture.

By asking your direct report questions, and by listening to them, you may then understand their train of thought and why they did it. For example, on one particular day, I was in the middle of a live call evaluation with one of my agents. During the recording, I heard the following take place between my agent and the caller.

The caller had asked if he would get the same agent on the phone for further help, if he called back tomorrow. My agent mentioned they would be in training tomorrow and it was best to reference the ticket number, and that anybody could help them. After that call, I sat down with the agent and asked them a few questions. I asked, "What are your plans for tomorrow?" They said, "Nothing. I am working." So, I asked, "Are you in training tomorrow?"

They said, "No."

I said, "Well, I have a recording on your last call where you said, you would be in training tomorrow. I'm just curious about why you said that."

They said to me, "Okay, you got me. I was going to call out tomorrow, as my father is not doing well and is resting at home after having surgery. My brother was going to help tomorrow, but may not be able to." Let's re-cap on what just happened.

The agent was honest about the situation and I approached this by asking questions. I could have just told him what I found. But I didn't. I asked questions first. Also, in the end, I understood what was happening at home and why he did what he did. This was all done by listening and asking questions.

This had also turned into a coaching session with the advisor. I asked him to just simply tell me about the situation instead of just taking off. Especially in a call center. If I were to know the next day he could not make it in, I could have adjusted some schedules as needed to be in a better place for the next day. It's important that your team remains honest and lets you know of any concerns as soon as possible.

2. Avoid Tunnel Vision

My children love to visit the 'Ball Store.' This is known to us as: 'Target.' One of the things that my son, Nathan, is a huge fan of is the Teenage Mutant Ninja Turtles action figures. What we do on most weekends is look for new action figures that my son does not have. As of now, my son has up to over thirty action figures that he has collected.

During a visit to the 'Ball Store,' a leadership lesson was born through this experience. As we arrived at the store, my wife took Tabbi and Nathan to the movie aisle, and I took my daughter, Ursula, into the toy section to look for a new action figure for my son. As I'm looking through the various rows of action figures, I have 'Tunnel Vision.' I'm focused on finding something in this aisle that he does not have for his collection.

During this time, I lunged forward as something hit my leg and my daughter said, "Got you." As I turned around, I saw my daughter drop something that made a loud metal sound. She had struck my leg with an aluminum softball bat that she had found on the ground of the toy aisle.

How did this happen? This happened because I was oblivious and had 'Tunnel Vision' and allowed it to happen. This was lying in the aisle on the floor that I was in, and I missed it because I didn't notice it.

Think of this and how it applies to leadership. Often, we overlook things that are right in front of us. For example: one day, I was administrating a sit-in with an agent at their desk. The goal was to sit with them for a few hours and watch how they operated as an employee.

During my observation, I noticed there was a gold mine of things that I overlook every day. I bet you overlook things that are right in front of you as well. Like how during that day's sit-in, I noticed that the employee had many files on his PC and many things hanging up on his cube. I asked him about a particular file that he created and seemed to use on a few calls that day.

He told me this file really helped him identify if they were giving him the correct information.

It had prefixes that would confirm if the information the caller provided was correct, as many callers provide incorrect information. I asked him if he would mind sharing the file.

The file was quickly shared among the team and was able to help agents with the accuracy of their calls.

I challenge you to take a look at your team(s) and what resources they are using; such as files they have created and the significance of items they have hung up, and how it helps them throughout the day. There is a gold mine of information right in front of you.

If you currently are not sitting with your employee for a few hours on a daily basis, I would challenge you to do so. During this time, you will better understand the hidden gems of recourses they are using. Also, more importantly, you are able to see what they are doing during the down-time, and will have a conversation with them as a person and not a manager.

The biggest fear, I think, of employees is sometimes withholding information. The reason they might do so is because of job security. They feel that by providing this information to everyone, they become less valuable to the company. Like anything else, knowledge is power. But this knowledge needs to be shared among everyone and the employees need to understand this.

What is also interesting about this observation is how your employee internalizes information and the variance of information hung up by them. During your observations, take a quick notice of your employees and understand the simple principle of adapting to environments. For example: one of the things many organizations have tried—which has proven to increase productivity—is dual monitors for the employee.

This concept of dual monitors does, in fact, work. But take it one step further. If you had all the employees on a single monitor, and then gave everyone two, you would probably notice even the fair performers are able to do more with two monitors, right? That's true, but what you really want to watch is those who can thrive in less ideal conditions; those are your super stars.

What I mean by this is: go to your team (hypothetically, of course) and tell them the great news, "I'm taking away one of your monitors, today." Interestingly enough, if that were to happen, look again at who your super-stars are. It's the same ones as before you switched to dual monitors. Why? These are the folks who know how to adapt to change and thrive in less ideal conditions.

3. The Pearl necklace Equals (Learn It, Teach It and Apply It Principle)

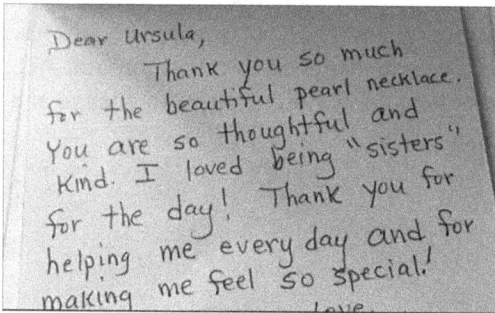

Dear Ursula,
      Thank you so much for the beautiful pearl necklace. You are so thoughtful and kind. I loved being "sisters" for the day! Thank you for helping me every day and for making me feel so special!
Love,

On one particular day, I noticed a note on top of my daughter's dresser. I opened the envelope, and realized I had never seen this note before. It looked like my daughter, Ursula, had taken this note out of her backpack and put it on her dresser. The image above is the actual note from her first grade teacher that was given to my daughter.

After reading the note, I was confused, because I did not give my daughter any pearl necklace for her teacher. At that point, I asked my wife about the note, and she asked, "What note?" After she read it, she told me she didn't give my daughter anything, either.

I called my daughter into my room and asked her where she got the pearl necklace from. My daughter told me she got it from Mommy's jewelry box, because she wasn't using it. This began a very interesting teaching lesson for my daughter.

We asked her how she would feel if we gave away one of her bracelets, which we had given her, to someone else. You don't have to wear it every day to like something. It's where the item came from that should be remembered.

After this event, I established the 'Learn It, Teach It, and Apply It' principle in leadership, which allows many things to happen. I want you to think about some of the challenges you have as a leader in your current role.

Think particularly about training and development. This particular topic can be difficult, due to training budgets, resources, etc.

This principle will help you mold your employee with little or no money, and more importantly, allow the employee to learn and teach others. Here is how I turned this principle into a conceptual idea, then into an actual finished result.

Conceptional Planning

First, you will need to develop a theme, and you will need to brand your project in order for it to remain consistent. I branded this the: 'Walking on Thin Ice – A Breakthrough Series'. The name, as it suggests, means you are walking on thin ice and are cautious as you cross the body of water encapsulated by the ice. You may fall in, but that's how we learn. *Learn It, Teach It, and Apply It principle.*

As a leader, you must set the tone of the assignment by having respected due dates. You can accomplish this through a white board or through other means.

Learn It Principle

The first thing for the 'Learn It' principle is to assign your employee a project they know nothing about. The idea is to assign them time to work on their project. I give about one month for them to work on their project, with 2-3 hours a day for them to develop content. They will build this project into a PowerPoint and will present it to our team in a team meeting.

During their scheduled time, they will start to build their project by reaching out to the known Subject Matter Experts (SMEs) and researching the issue. You might ask: "Why not just have an SME build a project since they know the content well?" That's a great question, and I have done it before, but there is a downfall in doing it that way. Yes, the SME is teaching others and gets a sense of accomplishment, but what did the SME learn? Nothing.

The Learn It Principle forces the employee to learn it and teach others. This is a great way to develop the skills of the employee, especially when the training budget is limited. Once the project is done, I will review it and ask for any last minute changes.

Teach It Principle

Next, in the 'Teach It' principle, we will establish a date in which they will present their project to the team. The employee is able to teach others about their project and provide handouts about their finished project to the team during the presentation. At the end, it's important to have the employee ask if anybody has any questions.

Apply It Principle

The last phase of this process is the 'Apply It' to the team. What I mean when I say 'Apply It' is for them to demo this project first hand. For this phase, I film the employee doing the project and post this video in front of the team during a team meeting, along with the brand title of the series: *'Walking on Thin Ice.'*

Benefits of All of These Principles:

- Builds confidence
- Learning/Development
- Sense of challenge outside of their normal activities
- Employee retention
- Sense of accomplishment

- Public speaking
- Free training – employee will train others
- Separation from regular work by given project time

During each of these projects, after each employee goes through the process, I ask them, "Do you feel you are now more confident with this subject?" All employees answer: "Yes."

In fact, these projects were so successful, that other departments and other tier levels are reviewing the contents, so that they can stay abreast with these topics and be ready to handle them when they move up in their development.

Since finishing these projects, we have started a library of them internal to our group. The most rewarding component of this whole process is seeing the employee learn and grow; but not just from doing the project. One of my direct reports told me prior to this project that he had never created a PowerPoint deck before.

He ultimately learned a new skill in addition to the new information he acquired from doing the project.

If budget restrictions are a concern, then this is the simple solution to involve the employee. Be a leadership hero, assign them a project using these principles, and thank me later.

4. What Defines Me

Often times, children surprise you with perhaps their choice in words, or in this case, with drawings, which can show their creative side. My daughter, Ursula, provided my wife with this drawing.

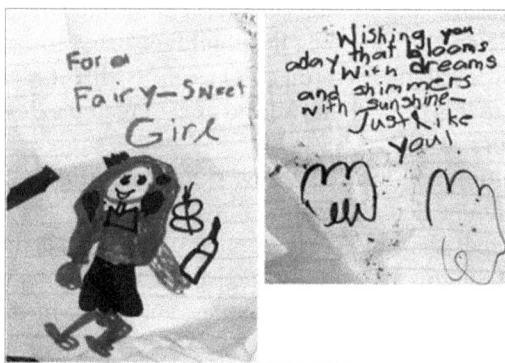

This drawing says: "For a Fairy-Sweet Girl." What's even more interesting is the choice of words used in the next drawing. After I read the full message, I knew for a six-year old there was no way she knew the words described on the second image.

So, I asked my daughter how she knew the words. Her response was not verbal. She handed me a Hallmark Greeting card that someone had given my wife many years ago. She had copied it word for word and had added her own touch with her own picture and clouds.

It's evident that my daughter loves to draw and has used her creativity to provide this piece of work. One day, Ursula came home with a nice, tidy book from her graduation from first grade, put together during the last few days of school.

It outlined her favorite thing to do at school, and many important events. This leads to the identities of your employees. Do they know who they are? Do you, as their manager?

Who Am I Paper

Look at your employees for a moment. Do you really know them outside of work? Do you know their hobbies and what inspires them personally and professionally? If you don't, then you must get involved with them in order to understand them better.

Most parents, like myself, know their children's hobbies, T.V. shows, and favorite thing to do right now. These simple things you know should be asked among your team. Raising children and managing employees should be treated equally. Do you really know your employees outside of work? Do you know their state of mind now and in the future? Use this basic technique to ask them these raw questions. It's harder than you think, but the outcome is something amazing.

The challenge is to ask your employees specific questions to learn more about them. This will help you to ask controlled questions and for them to really think about these questions. This is a great thing to do, especially with new hires joining your team.

During this process, I have employees tell me about challenges occurring in their life; whether they are personal or professional. I also find that employees will tell more in a letter, rather than verbally.

During this exercise, I've come across subtle clues that employees may want to become a manager by reading their paper. It is important that if the department has any future manager transfers, these papers are tucked away tidily in the employee folders. This will help the next manager with their career development. Employees feel more comfortable writing their feelings down on paper rather than explaining it verbally. The same applies to new hires that are being evaluated as temps. You may want to give them this paper to see what their state of mind is in that moment.

In the end, you will end up with a polished paper that provides more insight into the employee by doing this simple exercise. The paper is designed to challenge the employee, as well as the make the manager understand more about the employee.

Shown below is the 'Career Development Challenge,' that I provide to my employees.

On the next page is an example of a well-thought essay paper from an employee. As you can see, based on the control questions, it tells his story; and by reading, you learn more about the individual.

This is a simple task that you can assign your employees to easily learn more about them:

My name is Keith, which is derived from Scottish heritage and means "woods" or "of the Forest". It fits me well as I'm definitely the opposite of a city person. I live in a quiet suburb, and would live in a rural area if I could.

I'm inspired by The Constitution and the Founding Fathers. The Constitution is one of the greatest documents ever written. With the exception of Abraham Lincoln, I have yet to see leaders as wise and intelligent since. Professionally, I am inspired by knowledgeable coworkers. At my previous job and the short time I have been at   xxxxx   , it never ceases to amaze me the knowledge I pick up from my peers.

My passions encompass Photography, Films, Biking, and Computer technology. I am currently starting a project to digitize all my old family photos and home movies in order to make a central family history on the web.

What matters most to me right now is the state of our country and the not so inspiring political leaders we have, getting and staying healthy, paying off the debt I accumulated taking care of my Mother in her last years, and my recent year of unemployment.

My job is very important to me as it gives me the opportunity to learn and share what I learn with my peers. I particularly enjoy the challenge of learning a new breed of machines, and take great satisfaction when I am able to help a Field Tech resolve an issue.

Personal traits that I take pride in is my patience and listening skills. I enjoy listening to people much more than talking.

What excites me about the future are the opportunities for growth at xxxxx xxxxx . In my last job, there was no real possibility of advancement. The morale is also much, much better at xxxxx than in my last position. It is a fun place to work.

What scares me about the future are the political climate in the country and the changes in the Health care system. My personal health is of great concern to me and I am worried about the availability and quality of medical care in the future.

Last, as a show of respect to the art of sharing, it's only fair that you, as their manager, have something similar to share with them. I've had success in sharing a topic with my team.

The topic was: '*What Leadership Means to Me.*' In an essay, you, as a leader, should challenge yourself and write a piece that can be shared with your team about you. This will also help your authenticity with your team and will show them what inspires you every day.

Once you have finished your paper, present it to your team. This will go a long way and is a sign of trust. Here is an example of an excerpt from my own paper:

What does it mean to be a leader?

Have you ever been on a road trip riding with someone? For me I take notice of my surroundings, I look up at buildings and often find people staring back down at me, I notice things that generally people aren't looking at. That's what being a leader is to me, it's the ability to see things that aren't generally visible to the common eye.

Being a leader is about sincerely caring about your team professionally and personally. Being a leader is also about being a mentor to your team and eventually the right for your team to sincerely appreciate what you do. Often times I thank My team for the outstanding job they do but when your team thanks you that validates you as a successful leader.

I believe as leaders we must welcome adversity in open arms. Naturally we want things to run smoothly but sometimes when things turn sour that's a gift and opportunity for us to solve. Even if it's too late we still learn from what occurred and as a leader I thrive on any opportunity.

Another simple task, I would recommend in this chapter, is to have quotes on a wall at your workplace. Ask your employees, "What does this job mean to you?" Then, post all their responses onto a wall that is visible to everyone.

Lastly, share with them a quote about what leadership means to you, and likewise, post it on the 'wall of fame' as well.

My quote posted on the wall of fame is:

"Leadership is much like an unfinished art project. It is defined to a degree, but always a work in progress. In order to obtain one's attention, lines need to be drawn by using abstract colors." – Joe McGee

Finally, have the employee explain their quote to you and the meaning behind it. You will do the same with your quote, so that they understand your point of view.

Learn One Thing Exercise

I would recommend this exercise to drive home the point of knowledge sharing. The exercise, 'Learn One Thing,' asks the employee to list one thing that saves them throughout the day.

Have the employee present his/her topic in the next pre-huddle or team meeting. You will find others may not know this topic, and will gain knowledge by sharing with others.

An example of input from an employee could be anything from time or PC tips, or all the way to practical things to check or verify in your everyday work.

By doing this exercise, you will find great success in employees sharing secrets about their success and things that save them throughout the day. This will also open doors for more sharing and collaboration when these ideas are being presented.

Icebreaker Involving the Team

Another good icebreaker I would recommend, is a 'Who Am I?' guessing game among the team. Send out an e-mail communication and ask the same questions to your team.

In my example, I ask for the following information:

- My first vehicle
- My first job
- My favorite movie
- An interesting fact you may not know
- My favorite hobbies consist of…
- If I had the opportunity to meet a famous celebrity or athlete, I would meet…

Turn this into a PowerPoint and have fun by adding images to the deck that match the employee's answers.

Have some fun with this project and tidy it up into a PowerPoint file, then print the completed file out for your team. Next, break your group into smaller groups based on your team size, and have them try to guess what slide belongs to what employee. This is a dual-purpose ice breaker. This not only allows the team to work as a group, but also allows knowledge sharing and is a simple way to promote learning about others while having fun.

You will also be surprised that many in your department may not know anything about their neighboring co-worker, yet, they have sat near them for many years. It's now time to share information with others and start talking to your neighbor.

Mistakes, Respect, and Regret

During your career as a leader or an individual contributor, you will have bumps along the way; but it's about learning through these experiences. During my career in 2006, I worked as an individual contributor on a 'Level 1 help desk.' This type of environment had a lot of friction between level 1 and level 2.

On one particular day, one of the level 2 agents instant messaged me and asked me what I did in my notes of a ticket, as he was not clear on interpreting what I wrote. As I was on another call, I had messaged him back what I had reviewed with the customer. His reply back was "In English, please."

My reply was, "Give me a second, I'm on the other line. But I can explain it to you as if you were an eight-year old. I hope that's clear as crystal."

Later that day, he had informed my supervisor of what transpired. My supervisor of course, told me that was not professional. Now, of course, this was a mistake on my end. But later in my career, I had moved up to the level 2 team.

The person who was in charge of assigning influx tickets was the person I messaged that to. He never assigned me a single ticket and respected my bold statement.

The lesson here was that my bold stance allowed me to gain respect as I moved to another group.

Development Challenge

Another important challenge is to task your employee with committing to something, and to put it into writing for their development. For example: the questions below are something I want my team to ask themselves. The employees will commit to answering them on paper, so that they can grow through this experience. Once they commit to these, it will then become a mutual commitment between you, as their management, and for them, as an employee, to reach those goals.

Your Name: _____

Current Title: _____

1. Between now and 2 years from now (Your Name), _____ is committed to develop their skillset for their new role as (List the role you are interested in) _____.
2. In order to prepare for your new role, what do you need from others?
3. What specific commitments will you make to prepare for your new role?
4. As you enter into this new journey, what new skills will provide the biggest payoff?

Next, ask specific questions about their current role:

1. Currently in your existing role, are you performing your best work? Explain your job, your workflow, and any opportunities for improvement.
2. Where have you achieved your greatest successes in your current role?
3. What can you do better than anyone else?
4. What one thing impedes your performance?
5. If you had unlimited resources, what one thing would you do differently today?

Lastly, review this worksheet together during your next individual meeting, and mutually commit to these actions.

Signature Moves

If you look at sports, athletes develop a nickname, and more importantly, a signature move. If you follow professional football, then you know of the player who is known to have a 'Beast Mode.' He's known to be in 'Beast Mode' with his ability to rush and trample over his opponents; having a surge of energy.

Moving on to basketball, take a look at the Chicago Bulls—particularly from 1984 through 1999. We all know of number twenty-three and his famous signature move. While he was on the court, his signature move was sticking out his tongue as he drove his way to the basket. This was an indication that something magical was going to happen, and that he was going to score.

Take a look at your employees. What are their signature moves and/or what are they known for? Are these moves positive? Are they one-sided? Whatever they are, I would recommend identifying these qualities and working with the individual to pass that skill on to others. Whether it's knowledge, or the way they can develop work being in their element, it should be identified.

For me, my signature move has always been a trusted source of technical knowledge and patience. I am someone who is able to break through an issue by solving it and writing up solutions for others. I had a keen eye on turning problems into solutions, and people knew that I would be more than fine taking a ticket for a few days until it was resolved.

5. Show and Tell Is a Must

In many grade schools, 'show and tell' is a tradition carried on from many years with a simple task. The task is to bring something in to share with your class and to explain how it's important to you. For my daughter, first grade was no different, and the items brought in told a story. In order to acquire the attention of your team, I would recommend using objects or exercises to enhance the point you are delivering.

As an example coming from a phone call center, it's always a challenge to ensure training on all topics is covered, and when it's not, try to improvise on the spot with confidence.

One of the exercises—that I utilize to drive this point home—is the: 'Chair Wheel Drive' exercise.

Chair Wheel Drive Exercise

This exercise can be delivered during a team meeting or at an informal team gathering on the floor. First, ask for two volunteers and then assign them their roles. We are going to need a sales person and a customer for this exercise. The rest of the group will make observations on what is taking place, and we will get their input at the end.

Next, the sales person and the customer will both be handed the flyer below for the vehicle which is for sale:

Features:

- CWD (Chair Wheel Drive)
- 10 wheel independent turning system (chair design)
- Color: Paper Bag Brown
- Engine: 350CC power stroke engine with glide option
- Safety: Brown Bag Air Bag system; Self Parking
- MPG: 21
- Cargo Room: 2 passengers with unique roof design. Able to carry 250 pounds of cargo.
- Warranty: 3 year or 1000 miles whatever comes first

We are now going to implement some control words into this exercise. Have the customer pick two words, and the words that are selected are the control words. The customer will use these topics as reasons why he is not completely sold on the vehicle, and will then ask questions on these topics. It's the sale person's job to try to sell the vehicle, or at the least get contact information from the customer.

The exercise will end either when the vehicle is sold, or when the sales person gets their contact information, or simply when the customer declares they are not ready to buy. When the exercise is done, ask the team who was observing this for their thoughts on what happened during this exercise.

You will see that your audience will provide feedback of how uncomfortable the sales person was. He was handed a paper just a few minutes earlier and really didn't know everything about the product.

Think about this and how it applies to your support center. How many times do we get calls which have questions that we cannot confidently answer? From this point forward, individually, I want you to pay particular attention to the calls you do get, and that you have to do your best with the subject matter. Make a list of these calls, so that we can identify the areas where we can make you more confident and familiar with that topic.

Orgone Energy

One of the other exercises in which I use objects to illustrate a point is: 'Orgone Energy.' Orgone is a pseudoscientific and spiritual concept, described as an esoteric energy or hypothetical universal life force, originally proposed in the 1930s by Wilhelm Reich. In this object, you will notice metal shavings, copper, quartz, and many other elements. These elements are supposed to bring longevity.

During an informal gathering, I use this object and pass it around the room. I tell my team to feel the object, then I explain its origin. Like, when the item is close by, it's supposed to give a life energy to provide good health and to possibly prevent cancer. How many of us know the story behind quartz watches? Some are to believe that the quartz close to the skin transfers energy.

Next, I ask (knowing the history of this energy), "How many of you want to keep one and try it out?" All of my team drank the Kool-Aid. But why?

As frontline technical support employees, we must also wear a 'Sales Hat' at all times. We are going to be presented with issues that will be new and foreign to us.

It's about your pitch and sounding confident when you really don't know too much about the product. After this demonstration, I had members of my team approach me and ask if I made this stuff up. Whether I made stuff up or not—it sounding authentic and believable is what we must always do during the day; as you need to set the example and tone for your conversations to your employees. This is a good exercise to bring that point across to your teams.

6. The Element of Surprise

Yes, that's a picture of me posing as a fighter in a goofy outfit for my daughter. One of the things my daughter asked me when she saw a boxing event on T.V., was:
"What is the point of this?" I told her that boxing is like a chess match; a game which needs careful planning to defeat your opponent. A smart boxer needs physical training but also a solid mind to win the match.

If you watch closely, you will notice some boxers will show the same move and their opponent will pick up on that quickly. It's when you show your opponent one move, and then do something completely different, that the element of surprise wins the match.

In fact, my daughter did just that one night, and I was in for the 'Element of Surprise.' My daughter is usually pretty serious and does not mind telling anyone what's on her mind. However, one night, I was surprised by what she did.

She had climbed up on my bed as I was watching T.V. and started tickling my neck for no apparent reason. I asked her, "What are you doing?" She just laughed and continued to tickle my neck and face.

In doing so, I realized something magical had just taken place. My daughter was able to make me smile and laugh; a true element of surprise had just happened.

Now, think about this for a minute. Think about what you are currently doing for your teams to promote a fun and productive set of employees. Is it redundant, day in and day out? Have you not implemented the element of surprise? Are you too used to your routine? If so, you must change and give your team the element of surprise.

Easter egg Hunt

There are many things you can do to ignite passion in your team that doesn't cost anything. For example: one of the things my daughter loves during Easter is an Easter egg hunt. Let the childish imaginations ignite and do this for your team.

Recently, I did just that for my team. Right before Easter, I brought in some Easter Eggs for my team. I designed a game during my informal gatherings that allowed them to have fun, and more importantly: learn from the experience.

The way it worked was: I split my team into groups of 3-4 people, gave them their first clue, then handed them the Easter egg that had a printed clue inside it.

They were then to read the clue and go to the location they thought the answer was in, to find the next clue. My questions were designed to ask them questions about the company and/or products, or questions about their team mates.

This is a very simple way to invoke creativity among your teams and give them that 'Element of Surprise' that's needed to break the ice up during the day.

You can also do this not only on special events or days, but in everyday situations. For example: have you thought of incorporating good surveys for the week or month, and rewarding the employee?

Before any employees are in the office, tape gift cards under their chair and then recognize the employee for their excellent survey remarks. Read the surveys—exclude their name—and then have the employees go to their chairs and see if they won.

Next, have a 'wall of fame' with the employees' pictures and the surveys hanging on the wall.

Appreciation Week

You may also want to think about an 'Appreciation Week' for your department. In the planning of the week, you are to design special events to invoke your appreciation for their efforts. Do this event yearly.

Some of the events I have done for this week include:

1. Putting Tournament for Golf
2. Ice Cream Social Delivered Personally by the Management Team.
3. Raffle Prizes Drawn For Grand Prize
4. Cube Find (Design a game and have the employee guess what employee it is).
5. Company History Game
6. Management Team to Deliver Coffee Mug and Shirt.

The last touch would be to do something that really shows that your department is appreciated. I have done this in the past and it has a great touch on appreciation. Have the CEO of the company come and meet your staff, then shake hands and answer any questions. How many of us have met or talked to our CEO? This last personal touch goes a long way with your employees and shows that they are truly appreciated. This is especially important in fast-paced positions that can often be considered a "Thankless Job."

Join Me for an Interview

As many of us do as a hiring manager, we must interview new talent as part of our duties. In doing so, have you ever thought of asking one of your current employees to join you for the interview?

By doing so, you trust your employees for feedback and for them to ask their own questions during the interview. This is also important for job growth and to challenge your employee to do something they normally would not do.

The Old Switcheroo

If you are in a call center environment, then this is perfect for the 'Element of Surprise.' It's called 'The Old Switcheroo Challenge.' It allows you to partner up with a local charity organization and to have some fun as well.

The manager's envelope that raises the most money will have to take phone calls in the spirit of this exercise.

I have done this challenge in the past near Thanksgiving, and have raised money for families needing a meal for the holidays.

First, write up the challenge and distribute it to your team. With it, you are able to raise money for those in need and you will also have some fun with the management staff.

The management team is pleased to announce 'The Old Switcheroo Challenge.' This challenge will allow the employees to donate money to X charity group and will nominate your leadership member to take phone calls.

- This challenge will run from these dates (Determine the dates)
- Use the envelopes of the leadership team you wish to nominate to take calls, by making your donations to his/her name. Place the money into an envelope, then into the locked donation box in the front of the room.
- On X date, the donation totals will be added up and the leadership member with the most amount of money raised will be declared the winner. The winner

will be the one who will take calls one day in November.

- All the money raised, regardless of the winner, will be donated to X charity group.

Here is an excerpt from Food Share's website for the donation our team provided by doing this great exercise, as an 'Element of Surprise.'

Monday, November 11, 2013

Employees donate and have fun doing it! Joseph McGee stopped by today for a tour of our new facility, and to present the Food Share with $200.00 for their 'Switcheroo Challenge' fundraiser. Employees donated money and nominated a member of the management team to go outside of their usual job description and take incoming calls for a day.

---

7. Celebration Days Are Too Routine

My daughter asked me, "Why do we only have one birthday?" If you look into what this statement is saying, think about it for a moment. In our society, we are brought up to do something nice on selective days. For example, on all the days including but not limited to the days below we are doing something special:

- Birthdays
- Christmas
- Valentine's Day
- Anniversaries
- Baby Showers

If you think into this some more, why is our mindset conditioned to follow special days only? This pattern needs to stop and adapt into normal days. We need to follow our routine less in all that we do.

Why is it that for a great day to exist, we must follow a pattern of making that day special? The answer is quite simple: we are forced into these days simply because on a normal day, that's all that day means.

Why can't an ordinary day be something more? Why is gift exchanging only happening on forced days? We need to change this pattern and make an ordinary day into an extraordinary day, and not live by such patterns.

As a leader, we must break up the routine, because being too involved in the routine is a dangerous road to failure. How do you separate the day and not become too involved in your routine?

Some of the things I would recommend, would be to mix it up every day to ensure a good fluid moving day is set forth. For example: one day, get out of the office and have lunch off-site and not at your desk or at the café. The next day, keep it moving and do something different, whether it's a walk around the facility or maybe stop and visit another co-worker on another floor you have not seen in quite some time, due to your busy day. We must make our day different every day.

In your routine, you can involve the team and make a normal day be something memorable. Think for a moment of all the different companies in your state that are very similar to your own. You, probably right now, in fact, have some contacts at that company. Have you ever considered doing a field trip to visit that office and see what they are doing with their teams?

You may also be involved in other technical groups that have meetings across your state that you attend for development. Have you considered bringing your staff to such meetings for networking?

By involving your staff in off-site meetings, this is a perfectly FREE way to mold their development by networking and getting that time away from the office.

As leaders, we must find ways to turn routine days into special days; both for our growth and also for the growth of our teams If you think for a moment about what your current schedule is today and what you are doing, is it the same every day? Maybe, you go for a walk every day at noon. If that's true, then you need to mix it up and not become so routine.

Get Involved

Get involved and look into some of the things that your company has to offer, whether it's volunteer work or special programs. Does your company have a mentoring program? If not, maybe start one and do something special with your extra time during the day, and ultimately be less routine.

The bottom line is that if your team members (staff and other members of leadership) know where to find you at a certain time, then you follow your daily routine too much, and could be doing more to make the day its own special day and not just an ordinary one. These moments are out there, and we must act upon them.

Bring the Outside Within

Another good sticking point about sticking to your daily routine can be the way you present your meetings with your staff. Depending on the hot items and discussion, you may want to consider leveraging a non-bias, outside party to speak at your next team meeting to really drive that point home. This is a great way to have another non-biased person point of view give his/her perspective.

8. Understanding the Bigger Picture

My daughter often asks what a particular word means, or during homework assignments, she'll ask what the meaning of something is.

Think about the very basic concept of branding in your next team meeting. You may find it surprising that more than 80% of your team does not know what your company logo means and how it was developed for branding.

Recently, I did just that and asked my team if they knew what the logo they wore on their shirt meant. I was surprised that my team did not know what the logo represented, or the meaning of it.

This is a great opportunity to give a history lesson about your company, so that your employees know the meaning of your company. How do you think they would feel if they were stopped by someone and asked about the company and the meaning of the logo? If they don't know how to answer those questions, are they truly invested in the meaning of the company?

One of the other popular questions is, "How do I fit into the organization as an individual contributor?" Do they know the organizational structure and how our department aligns with the Bigger Picture? If they do not know, then this is the time to catch them up to speed with these facts.

Knowing these facts, an employee should feel more appreciated in their alignment of the group and must be able to be more productive knowing that their small or big tasks make a difference. You must paint a line that may not be visible for them to see the difference. When you do paint a line for them to understand, you could put it into a graphical chart, which is visually appealing to the eyes and easy to understand.

We can approach the facts with stories and the ability to deliver the stories to your team, so that they can understand the importance of their every day job.

Have you ever been on a road trip with someone? For me, I take notice of my surroundings. I look up at buildings and often find people looking back down at me. I notice things that generally people aren't looking at. That's what being a leader is to me; it's the ability to see things that aren't generally visible to the common eye.

On one particular day, at a traffic light, as I was appreciating the fine lines of the building curves and structural elegance, I noticed a little boy n a window about four floors up. As I looked up, he noticed me and waved that day, and I waved back.

During that day, there were probably hundreds of cars that traveled through that intersection, but how many of us noticed that little boy?

This is much like your job that you do day in and day out. How many people, other than me, might notice what you do first hand? Probably not many, since I interface with you directly. But this does not mean you go unnoticed by the bigger picture.

Now, the little boy was probably looking outside the window for many of the same reasons. He was looking for appreciation and acknowledgement outside of his family. Did he get it on that particular day when I noticed him? Yes, he did.

9. Strangers Are Among Us

One day, at a local store we were checking out, my daughter noticed a man behind us. She said quite loudly, "Daddy, that's a bad man behind us." I asked her why she thought that, and she told me he was a stranger. I had to explain to my daughter that in this world, there are strangers; but not everyone is a bad apple.

I told her to think about a few things for a second. "Remember the time when we went to the amusement park and we had to "share" a ride with people we didn't know? They started to talk to us, remember? They were with their family. Did you think they were bad people?"

She said, "No."

"It's okay to talk to strangers when adults are present. Not everyone is bad," I explained to her.

I told her to think about Halloween. What happens on Halloween? We are gathered to dress up and go to strangers' homes for candy with an adult. We are going to houses that we have never been to before, and are quite simply, interacting with strangers.

From a leadership perspective, think about your company with the many different departments it has. Do you know any of the other management staff? Or do you just know the management staff among your department? I bet your answer may be limited to only one or two departments. It's time to stretch your legs and realize that strangers are among us.

It's these strangers who are other managers working for the same company as you. What struggles and things are they going through in their department? It's time to get to these other departments and realize it's okay to talk to other strangers in the management.

By seeking other business segments of the company, it's time to identify these managers and work on similar challenges that you are facing.

For example: I recently attended a leadership conference and found many different leaders within my own company, who I, to this day, remain in close contact with. This is a great way to also develop your own personal development with the new people you just met with.

Personal Development Growth

As we all have our own goals individually, we must challenge ourselves, so that we get to where we want to be in our career. Along the way, we will meet new people and be in strange and unfamiliar territory.

For example: my journey for success has always been doing the following, so that I would stand out from my peers. I call this the: 'McGee Success Ladder':

The McGee Success Ladder

1. Do more than what's expected.
2. Understand the role and then beat the snot out of it.
3. Show the value of your work through projects and willingness.
4. Get something assigned to you? Do it, immediately. If you face a road block, go after it and NOT around it.
5. The most important one is to go outside of your comfort zone.
6. Always be one step ahead as a contingency plan.

During my career, I have been able to get what I want by setting goals and having a strategic plan of how to get to that role.

Now, the biggest mistake people can make is about how people deal with not getting the role they want. For example:

if you don't get the role you expected to get and someone else got it, you should be asking your boss one simple question. It's all about the approach and how you are taking the news of defeat. But don't let defeat beat you; come up with a plan to prove your value.

The questions you should be asking your boss are:

o   What specific skills did you like?
o   What specific skill sets should I improve?
o   What were my shortcomings that influenced the decision?

Often, we let our defeat get the better of us and may take it personally, and what do we do? We start comparing ourselves to the candidate who got it. We then start a conversation with your boss about why you are better than him and how it was the wrong decision. All of these things are not the right thing to do.

Don't be a stranger to others' success. It all starts with a plan and you can conquer any hurdle you are faced with.

10. Swimming with Sharks Is a Must

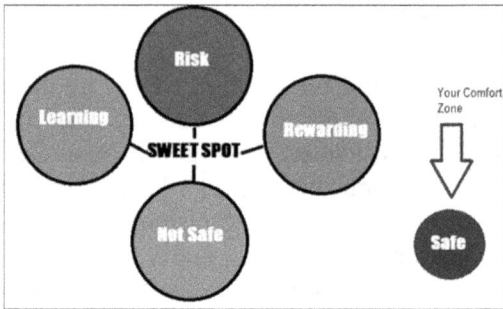

My daughter often asks why I do the things I do. Why am I involved in after-work events? The answer is quite simple: my involvement is to challenge myself and be involved in something great. My daughter loves to draw and is quite the artist. I've told my daughter to find something she does not know, learn it, and then do it. She hasn't taken on something foreign and different, yet. But I hope one day, she will.

How often as leaders do we go outside our comfort zones? In order to grow as leaders, we must do this at every chance that is presented, so that we can mature our skillsets and keep our minds fresh. We must be in the middle in the 'Sweet Spot' for success.

If we remain in our safe spot, and keep doing what we are doing, regardless if we do it well or not, that's not challenging yourself and it's a disservice to your growth. From this day forward, I challenge you as a leader to start 'Swimming with the Sharks' and remain in the 'Sweet Spot.'

For example: in my career, I consistently push the envelope, knowing that the core values shown below would be tested:

1. Risk
2. Reward
3. Learn
4. Not Safe

I started as a technical support advisor and quickly moved up the ladder. This, of course, was due to my ambitious goal-oriented mind and tactful planning of how to be noticed. Back in 2006, I worked as a technical advisor for a call center. This was all new to me and in fact, I never had done phone support before. My past experience from that point was more face-to-face interactions.

Early on in this role, my goal was to be noticed by the management, and I wanted to be number one on the performance list. Within a month, I was the top performer and was noticed by the management for my charismatic phone experience and the ability to resolve and multi-task. I kept asking for more projects and was quickly promoted to a trainer position within the organization.

I had never been a trainer before, but quickly planned out what I should cover with all new employees. Soon, I was remote training other employees around Canada and was working with the other training locations.

In 2009, moving forward was when I really wanted to challenge myself even more and wanted to find ways to be noticed as a valuable asset. Soon, I was sent over to work for Executive Desktop Support, in which I supported the legal team and high-level executives within the company.

During this time, my manager asked our team who would want to support the new CEO directly. I quickly raised my hand and was the only one who volunteered. This is an example of a risk. What if I failed to support the CEO of the company? For me, failure is not an option and we must take on challenges. As time went on, I was supporting the CEO and making him happy and it was self-rewarding to conquer this task successfully.

Jumping ahead to 2012, another challenge presented itself for an opportunity that I needed to jump on immediately; when I was in a management role for a call center. Our management team was preparing a revised document for our new hire quiz for the staff. It had been outdated and needed to be revised with specific content.

The content that needed to be in the quiz was the following topics:

1. PC Technical Questions
2. Networking Questions
3. Electrical/Electronic Questions
4. Mechanical Questions.

Knowing that I would be good and familiar with the PC, networking questions, and the other questions, I knew I had to go outside my comfort zone and make this into something amazing. I volunteered to take on this project.

Going into the project, I did some research and created questions along with answers for the revised document. After completing about 50 questions, I was now ready to show the document to the management staff. I explained the questions and answers, and asked, "Does anybody have any issues or changes for this document?" The answer was, "No."

My work and research had paid off, as I created a document that was flawless and ready to be distributed as the new version of the new hire assessment. This feeling and sense of accomplishment felt like the butterflies you experience when riding a roller coaster for the first time.

In 2014, I joined the CT HDI Chapter as VP of Social Media, and quickly assisted the board with many accomplishments. One of the things I wanted to do after taking over, was to give the brand a new look. I decided to re-brand the entire website and acquire hosting service and email accounts. Later on, that year, I decided to re-brand the newsletter formatting, so that it would stand out to our members and gave it an overhaul. Our members noticed the new website and gave me positive kudos for the work I had done.

For many that don't know about the Local HDI Chapters, it's a volunteer group that provides networking throughout your state by providing meetings for our members that cater to technical and service professionals. If my volunteer service was not enough, I still wanted to do more for the chapter.

In 2016, the post of president was up for elections and I knew I had the opportunity to challenge myself further by taking on this role for our chapter. If you are not challenging yourself now, I would recommend you to start looking for ways to do so, like I did. It's a must to keep your mind moving and working to be even more successful in all that you do.

11. Eyes on Me

My daughter asked me what she could buy with two dollars. I asked her where she had gotten the money from, and her answer was not something I expected. She told me one dollar came from my mother and the other dollar came from Mommy's dresser drawer. I said, "Ursula, that's called: stealing."

She said, "It's called: taking. It's okay to take from family."

The only way for her to understand is to put the explanation in terms that only she would understand. I asked her how she would feel if I gave away her favorite bracelet.

On a separate occasion, I noticed while checking out at the store, that my daughter was acting very suspicious. When I took her out of the carriage, I understood why. In lifting her out of the carriage, I noticed a bump in her pants and felt something. She had stolen a lip balm and placed it in her underwear. I told her if she wanted something, she should ask.

I asked her if she wanted her favorite store—which is Target—to close. She said, "What do you mean?" I told her millions of dollars are lost because of stealing, and it can cause companies to close their doors. I told her that people also go to jail for stealing items, and I asked if that was what she wanted. My wife's approach was sterner than mine, as she told her to stop or she was going to hell.

One of the items, we as leaders, should always be aware of is employees cheating the system. Do you have the appropriate reporting structure to see everything your employee is doing? Are you looking at everything?

If you are only looking at one metric, look again. There are many opportunities that an employee may short change the day by doing things that may go unnoticed for periods of time. In running a call center, you will run into many agents who think they can beat the system. I have classified them below.

The Shifter

One of the things that I eventually caught was: the shifting of AUX modes. The employee would go from Available Mode to ACW, then back to Available Mode, so their place in line would fall last instead of, possibly, first. They clearly found a way to cheat the system. But if this is something you are not looking at, then they will continue to do it.

The Busy Worker

This is seen when the agent lets the customer go, but the line remains open. The agent is not talking to anyone, and it would appear they are either still on a call or in AUX mode; depending on your call software.

The Outbound King

This can be seen where the agent is making excessive outbound calls. Are they calling back the customer, or making fake calls to remain busy? Perhaps they are calling their own voicemail, or are making personal calls to create the illusion that they remain busy.

The Punch out King

This is seen in agents who are oriented on leaving on time. They have a call they just got, but want nothing to do with it. They then just simply re-queue the call back to the phone skills, instead of going through with it.

The Disappearing Agent

This is seen where the agent is in an AUX mode incorrectly, such as: ACW or in a meeting, and are actually in the bathroom or on a personal break using the wrong mode.

The 'Please Hold' Agent

This agent would use the hold option to handle a disgruntled customer and just make them stay on hold, instead of diffusing the situation and calming them down correctly.

The 'Fix the World' Agent

Like most call centers, we generally tackle one problem at a time for obvious reasons, such as talk time, along with handling the incoming call load.

The 'your problem is my problem' agent will look for multiple issues and try to fix the world, instead of following the correct procedures.

The 'Fake Name' Agent

Often times, a bad call will occur and it may or may not be the agent's fault. At the end of the call, the customer wants to know who they spoke to. The agent then gives a fake name, hoping they would not get a bad survey against them.

The Call Out Agent

The agent calls out either on a Monday or Friday, consistently, in the hopes nobody will notice.

The 'I Worry About Me Only'

This agent thinks that 'with certain metrics in place, I don't want to skew my numbers, so I'm not going to help any team members with questions.'

The Knowledge Hoarder

This agent worries about job security and does not share any documents they created to be more productive. They hide and keep all the information to benefit themselves.

The 'Don't Do More' Attitude

This agent will not take on any additional work. This agent will only do the bare minimum and nothing more.

The 'Rules Don't Apply To Me'

This agent has been a veteran for many years and feels as if they can do what they want, and that the rules don't apply to them because of their years of service at the company.

If you have any of these personality traits at your call center, it's now time to let them know that 'the eyes are on them', and to start changing their bad habits into good habits.

12. Productivity Starts With the Environment

During vacation, my foot was an attraction for a group of fire ants that decided to attack it. My daughter asked me why so many of them were in a group. I told her they work together to be productive. I told her that if a group of them ever fell into a pool of water, they would stick together like a floating device in lieu of survival.

If you look at your current environment, what kind of perks do the employees have that will ignite their creative side? This is what you also need to look at. While being at work should be a serious task, there needs to be a balance that allows team work and a casual atmosphere for a better experience.

For example: did you know that Google employees have a relaxing setting from some examples shown below

1. Slide down a slide and relax in a new way to get down from a top floor.
2. Game room for the employees
3. The endless free food and snacks
4. Bring your pets to work
5. Reimbursement of up to $5000 to employees for legal expenses
6. Maternity benefits of a maximum of 18 weeks off at about 100 percent pay. The father and mother of the newborn are given expenses of a maximum of $500 for take-out meals in the initial 3 months they spend at home with the baby (Take-Out Benefits).

7. Financial support for adopting a child (Google's Adoption Assistance)
8. On-site car washes, oil change, bike repair, dry cleaning, gym, massage therapy and hair stylists are available at the company's headquarters in Mountain View, CA.
9. At the Googleplex, there's an onsite doctor, free fitness center, trainer, and facility to wash clothes among other benefits

Now, this list seems impossible for most companies, but there are always one or two things that can go a long way to make the environment more positive.

For example: one of my past employers had a ping pong table available to the employees during off-time for them to play. This allowed great sportsmanship and team-work; to start a tournament and keep your mind off work related items.

I have seen other environments with an in-house library for the employees to utilize and read as a group or individually, which definitely helps the employees' mind during off-time. Whatever works for your department, find that "something" to allow a more productive environment.

Other things that seem to work well are: group reading sessions in a circle on the floor. Start with a book and read together for 15-30 minutes a day. These are all small things that can help shape a better experience.

While on the topic of reading, one of the good things you can use in an interview is to ask the potential candidate, "What was the last book you read?" and "What did you learn throughout the book?". This will give you an idea of their interests and how they interpret a message.

If you are able to make decisions that influence a better working environment where the employee can be surrounded by a creative and safe environment, it is worth the investment.

The last thing you want to do is: create a 'Sweat Shop' environment that gives a negative feel. There are even small things you can do to provide a thank you or perk to your environment, such as (but not limited to):

1. Cater food by shutting down support and providing a 'thank you' meal.
2. Provide a BBQ and have games and activities for the employees.
3. Have a celebrity karaoke sing off. Your teams are the celebrities.
4. Allow off-time for birthdays
5. Set up a break room for the employees.

Based on the information above, if I was to give you a Google employee and give them your employee, what do you think would happen? What employee would be more creative? As you can see, there is always room to change the working environment for it to become a better place.

13. Answering Without Being Robotic

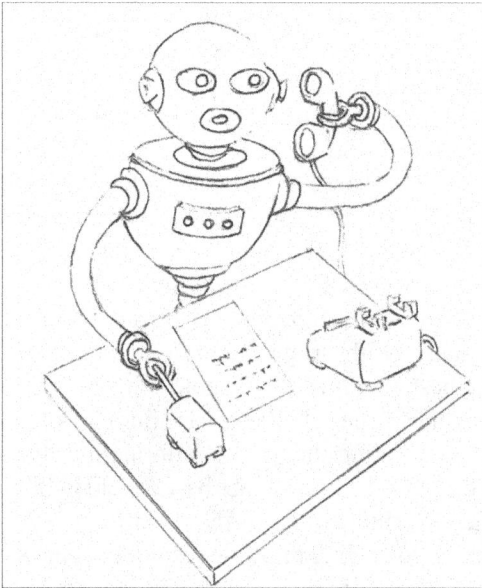

How many of us have attended a school play or a school concert?

These events can be performed due to well-rehearsed practices over many days and many hours. What's occurring is the internalization of information stored in a centralized place in our mind.

When it comes time for the actual event to take place, this information is then recalled and acted out just as they imagined. This is no more than learning a script; but what are we getting out of this exercise? No more than just scratching the surface without knowing the true meaning. I have seen my daughter perform a song for kindergarten that she worked hard on, but like anything else, this fading internalization will go away from non-use. What they are learning is no more than an internalization of words and timing—nothing more beyond that.

I'm a firm believer that if you have decided to do any scripting, you also must know what you are preaching. When one turns into a robotic reader, it's evident that the confidence and lack of delivery is no more believable than a talking duck.

Think about employee training for a moment. How many organizations will pay for certification boot camps and testing of certifications? In doing so, is the employee just simply internalizing the information with hopes of a book passing grade? We must also challenge them practically, to ensure they are not just book smart, but more importantly, they understand fully the skill they learned.

To have a successful, non-robotic team, we must all be consistent in how we deliver a recommendation or resolution. This all starts with a proper ITSM tool and a strong knowledge base that tracks all viable solutions.

Often times, the challenge is finding yourself in a quadrant of providing the correct information. For example: often, we don't find a knowledge base article with the answer, but instead, we find historical data that may be useful. The danger turns into finding multiple resolutions that steer you in different directions. In the end, this will lead the agent to their best judgement in what they think is the answer when multiple resolutions are discovered.

When this does happen, consistency among the team is skewed due to the uncertain decisions you must make.

Think about this for a minute when this situation does arise. If I had multiple agents taking the same call with multiple decisions to make, without a clear answer, what do you think the ratio is for agents giving the same recommendation? As you could imagine, it's going to be all over the place.

Consistency Is the Master Key

Let me ask you a few questions:

1. You are driving your vehicle on a dark road and are turning around a bend in the road. As you come around the corner, you notice a family of ducks crossing the road. What's the first thing you do?
2. You give a newborn baby a bottle of milk. What does the newborn baby try to do?
3. A cat falls into a swimming pool. What does the cat try to do?

Of course, while driving down a road, when you are presented by a group of ducks. You slow down or apply the brake pedal. When giving a baby a bottle of milk, the baby will drink the bottle. Lastly, the cat will try to swim or climb out of the pool.

The question is: why do all of these things happen? It's a natural instinct is the answer. This is the key for success; the answers our employees give come naturally and are consistent across the board.

In order to have your checks and balances in order, you must develop a decision factor system that all employees consistently follow without sounding robotic. The biggest mistake is allowing a consulting company to take over your support structure with just using a simple decision factor, without any technical knowledge. The only way your center will survive is to have a combination of a strong decision factor system, along with the proper training to answer questions outside the factor tree. If you do not, then your customers will see right through your staff's lack of knowledge.

14. Fear Is for Suckers

Not too long ago, my daughter asked me about getting a pet, and asked if I ever had any pets before. I told her that the only pets I had were real scorpions.

Many may not know this, but scorpions are nocturnal—meaning, they are only active at night. One of the species that I collected was: a 'Black Tip Fat Tail.' The scientific name is *Androctonus Australis*, and it is a hardy desert scorpion from North Africa, Somalia, the Middle East, Pakistan, and India. *Androctonus Australis* has very potent venom and is one of the world's most dangerous scorpions, due to its relative toxicity and temperament. During my peak, I had over ten different types of scorpions from all around the world.

Above: Androctonus Australis (Black Tip Fat Tail)

Another species that is deadly that I collected was nicknamed the 'Deathstalker'. The deathstalker (*Leiurus quinquestriatus*) is a member of the Buthidae family. The name *Leiurus quinquestriatus* roughly translates into English as "five-striped smooth-tail." The deathstalker is regarded as the most dangerous species of scorpion. Its venom is a powerful mixture of neurotoxins; with a low lethal dose.

Above: Leiurus quinquestriatus (Death Stalker Scorpion)

One of the questions I am asked often is why collect such risky specimens. Many may not know this, but I was interested in snakes and scorpions as a kid, but yet, I feared them. My thought was in life, running away from something and being afraid of something you don't understand is something you can change. So, get up and do something about it.

Not only did I want to handle a scorpion, but I wanted to handle the deadliest in the world and conquer my fear. The biggest mistake people are unaware of is: that scorpions don't have a vertebra and moving them with tweezers is a big mistake, as they can spin and sting you. My cautious approach is to use a deli cup and a long object to hit their tail and allow them to run into a deli cup. Then close the lid to secure them. An interesting fact is: scorpions glow green under a fluorescent black light.

Another interesting fact is: generally, the larger the, pincers the less deadly; as it relies on crushing its prey as opposed to stinging its prey. As you may notice, a lot of movie productions use the 'Emperor Scorpion' (shown below), simply because it's proven to be docile and less prone to sting, which makes it very safe to use.

Above: Pandinus imperator (Emperor Scorpion)

This is a large black scorpion, but it will rarely sting. I have also collected this scorpion.

In life, think about what you are afraid of. Is it physiological? Are you afraid of something, just because of how it looks, even though you have never experienced your fear first hand? What are you going to do about it? Are you ready to conquer your fear and face it head-on? I believe that for growth—personally and professionally—we all must face our demons and beat them. I strongly believe I have been able to succeed, by practicing this method of breakthrough. I strongly urge everyone to really fight your fears and tell a story through that experience.

In most technical call centers, you will notice two types of personalities. What I refer to as 'Experienced' and 'Strategic.'

Let's talk about scorpions. They hunt at night with small sudden moments, as they seek prey by moving in timed spurts. They are classified as an experienced hunter. Often times during the day, they find a spot and will only attack when provoked.

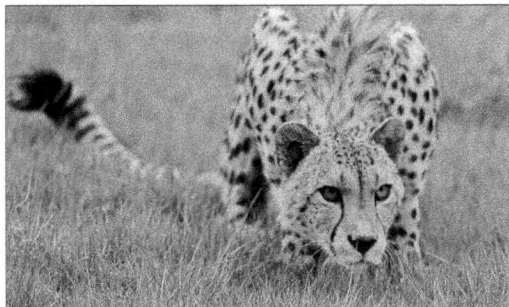

Think about a cheetah for a moment. They actively pursue their prey and are very strategic hunters.

Let's look at the different personalities in relation to a call center.

Experienced (The Scorpion)

These are the kind of staff who know their job and will only do the bare minimum. When the day is slow, they don't actively look for work. They do other personal related items, such as: surfing the internet or sending text messages, etc. They have been around a long time and know the hidden spots and know how to play the system.

I'm sure you have heard the tale of the frog and the scorpion. The scorpion asked the frog to carry him across the river, and the frog asked, "How do I know you won't sting me?" The scorpion replied, "Why would I do that, as we would both drown?" So, the frog agreed. Halfway across the river, the scorpion stung the frog. The frog asked him why he did it, since now, they would both die, and the scorpion replied, "It's in my nature."

This is meant to illustrate that some behavior is simply natural and will happen no matter how an animal or person is treated. The experienced worker has been around long enough to be stagnant in all they do. However, there are ways we must use to motivate these types of workers.

Ways to Motivate the Experienced Workers

How do they handle a call that they don't know much about? Are they attempting to find an answer? Or do they throw their hands up with an "It's not my problem" attitude?

Do an experiment and give them something they normally wouldn't do. How are they handling it? If they won't attempt it, then the only wake-up call for them is something you must do.

1. Align them up with a strategic worker. These workers are hungry and ready to prove their worthiness.
2. Give them a goal plan of what you expect them to do, and hold them accountable.
3. Let them know they are the model employee and need to set the example.

Without a goal or action plan, you won't get any more from the experienced workers. Set the pace and understanding sooner than later.

Strategic (The Cheetah)

These are typically the employees who are looking to prove their worthiness. You would see this particular characteristic in a fairly new employee who is looking to move up. They are hungry for success. Their characteristics are typically workers who find ways to be useful when they have down time. This is done by writing new ideas for improvement to the management, or by following up on e-mail or customer inquiries. They will also typically involve management and ask them for any projects or work they can help with.

Ways to Motivate the Strategic Worker

We must not hold these workers back in what they want to accomplish. These workers are ambitious and goal-oriented. They may not often know what they want. As I mentioned earlier in Chapter Four: "What Defines Me", we must mutually agree to a development plan for the employee. This is crucial in developing their skill set and more importantly, retaining the employee at the company.

As leaders, we must identify those two personality traits and take action, so that they perform correctly and the action is taken for their career path and growth.

My daughter did not know that I had collected scorpions as my pets. Soon, she had learned why I collected them and about the fear that was conquered by doing so.

This led her into working on one of her fears of being afraid of the dark. She's doing much better with the dark and has come a long way by combatting this sign of weakness; which is my definition of fear.

Fear can be broken with the right motivation. We all have fear, and this emotion can be combatted.

Above: Leiurus quinquestriatus (Deathstalker Scorpion) in Black Light

15. It's The Way You Use It

To expand on Chapter Four: "What Defines Me", it's the way you use it that really tells a story of growth and development. In school, my daughter strives for a "gold" rating, which is the highest rating for being helpful and doing the right thing. When she has not received the 'gold rating,' she works on the way she does things to become 'gold' again.

Much like in leadership, ways to show and motivate staff in key areas of improvements should be presented in a certain manner, so that the employee can work on the areas they need to improve on. The way you use your skillset is the most important when it comes to creating that winning team.

For example: every month, you should be sitting with your employee. In doing, so you're probably reviewing the KPIs and other elements for the employee's growth. The way the information is displayed is an important factor to ensure the employee sees how they are doing from the previous months and where they are going.

This can be provided in a graphical format, as shown on the next page. It's important that you show where the employee was, where they are today, and where they are going. This sets the pace for exactly knowing their expectations. This should not be done in an e-mail; you must sit with the employee and review the information.

Having this data available in a tracking method will save you time during performance reviews. You won't be scrambling for numbers, as it's already available for you.

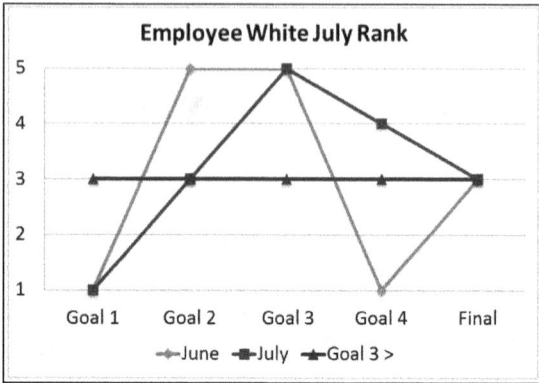

Employee White July Rank

Goal 1, Goal 2, Goal 3, Goal 4, Final

→ June ■ July ▲ Goal 3 >

Working on Areas of Improvement

By showing the employee's progress, it enables you to track and show areas of weakness; and it's documented for them clearly during the meeting.

Let's say, for example: the employee is the 'Fix the World Agent', as we learned about in Chapter Eleven. This agent clearly is not working in the realm of talk time and is only concerned and focused on resolving the issue no matter what.

In your conversation with them, it's the perfect way to show them how they are not following the procedure and the result of what happens when they do this.

For example:

1. Calls are in queue waiting to be answered, because you're too focused on solving the issue.
2. By doing this, how many times are you NOT fixing the issue and just wasting many minutes by dragging your feet?

This agent needs to understand the bigger picture and you need to ensure that they understand what they are doing is not the right thing to do.

You can fix this by pairing them up with an agent that knows when to let go, and see how they approach that. Give

76

them time to see how it should be done and encourage them to change.

After doing this, be sure to document your conversation and expectation, along with a date for change to take place. Write this in an e-mail and send it to the employee. The employee needs to understand the expectations of what they can do better.

One of the challenging things we are faced with is to change the meaning of calling a 'meeting' with the employee. More often than not, the employee thinks it's a bad thing, and that meetings are only called for things they did wrong.

Instead, we must also meet the employee a few times a month and praise the good feedback they are dying to hear. This can be accomplished by using my 5 and 5 principle in the next chapter. For example, perhaps surveys are coming in to state what a good job they did. This is a perfect time to showcase how good they are, and it's important they know and see that.

In your meetings, it's crucial to ask the employee if they have anything they want to bring up during your meetings. Find out what's on your employee's mind, so that it's not forgotten, and most importantly, document what was said. The last important factor is to have the employee sign off on your meeting, so that it's documented that you actually did meet. One of the other things you may consider doing as well, if HR allows, is to record your session for coaching purposes. This way, everything that was said and occurred during the meeting is documented.

When data is coming in, it's also very important we get it to the employee right away. Let's say, we just implemented a new template within our ITSM tool and the employee has not used it for the entire month.

We are finally meeting them after 30 days to tell them that they are using the wrong template. Why, as managers, are we not spot checking and catching this sooner than later? We need to coach them in that moment, instead of after the fact. It's the way you use the data in that moment that should be an important factor of coaching.

16. 5 AND 5

5 and 5...It's not a cocktail
Coach better using this concept...

Do your children need to be motivated in order to be rewarded? Start pushing them to do more and track these changes. This is much like the 5 and 5 concept you can do with your team. It starts with a chart, in which you put any item you want your children do, and then come up with a system of how many 'good' things they do; and track it with stickers.

If they hit a goal for each category, you can let them know what they will be rewarded with. It does not have to be about getting a toy or a DVD for them, as other things work as well. For example: a sleep-over at grandmother's house or a trip to a corn maze, etc.

This is when I discovered how to use the 5 and 5 concept, based on the same principle that I use at home. No, it's not a cocktail. The 5 and 5 coaching model is a simple principle to identify up to 5 items the agent is really good at throughout the month, but to also identify some shortcomings they need to work on.

How many times have you called an employee to a meeting and their reaction was, "What did I do, now?"

This happens more than you know, and we need to re-establish what the purpose is for a meeting with our employees for coaching.

As shown below, it is a great tool to use for coaching sessions for this dual purpose meaning of all the good and all of the items to improve on. The goal is for the agent to work on the items you identified for improvement, and for these items to shift to the positive side for the next month.

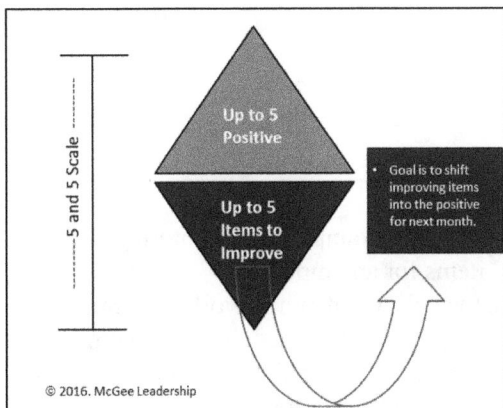

Up to 5 Positive

Up to 5 Items to Improve

-5 and 5 Scale

Goal is to shift improving items into the positive for next month.

© 2016. McGee Leadership

Next, spell out the positive things and give specific examples of what they did under each item on your chart. Be sure to give the items for improvement action goals, so that the employee understands what they need to do moving forward.

In the below example, the top portion shows the following 'positive' examples:

1. Mentor
2. Planning
3. Follow-up

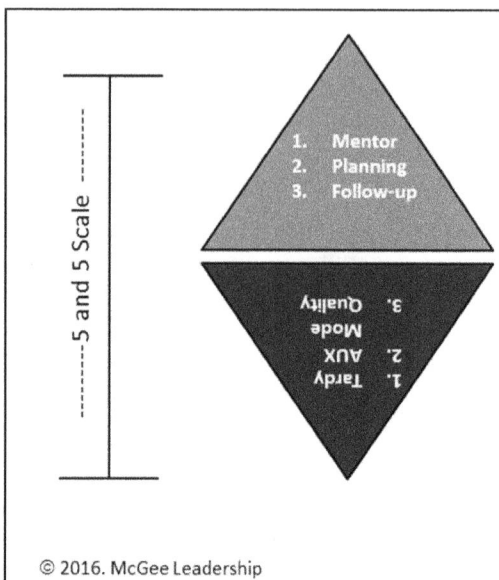

5 and 5 Scale

1. Mentor
2. Planning
3. Follow-up

1. Tardy
2. AUX Mode
3. Quality

© 2016. McGee Leadership

Below is an example of Mentoring for one of the 'positive' items for an employee.

While I watch Agent White work, he reminds me of many things. Have you ever watched the GMC commercial?

A pitcher who can paint the corners is known as a "Rembrandt" with the tag line 'Precision Matters'. Have you ever seen an orchestra guide the music in a well-timed fashion?

These are all examples of what Agent White represents, and that is the ability to provide guidance to others while handling his workload in a precise fashion. The reason that I compare Agent White to an orchestra or a precision of a fastball is because their vision of helping people while they are on the phone is remarkable. Agent White is able to multi-task, and they mentor others while they are on the phone helping someone. This agent does this every day and is able to multi-task with precision.

When they are asked to help others, or when they do a particular task, it's more often than not that they already know about it before I tell them. This agent's attention to detail shows they know what calls are in queue and they know what they are before I do. Agent White's strong work etiquette and multi-tasking ability makes them a true team player.

In the same fashion, also give specific examples along with a goal for any of the improvement items. Let's use "quality" for the example to improve on.

Your call audit score for January was 92%, which is lower than the 96% or greater expectations. The following items contributed to missing the satisfactory ranking for January are:

- Improper greeting
- Verbal items not in written ticket
- Missed items given to the agent

Your goal for February is to be 'satisfactory' or higher while keeping these items in mind above.

By using the '5 and 5' concept, you will benefit in the following ways:

1. Employee/Manager are on the same page regarding items to improve on and items they are doing well for each month.
2. These items are documented and reviewed together each month face to face.
3. By sharing both positive and improvement items, the employee's mind-set will change about a meeting being just about the 'bad things.'

17. A Walk Through Memory Lane Must Last Forever

How many of us have experienced a tenured employee get ready for retirement? An employee with over 30 years of service has called your workplace their second home and are now ready to give it up.

I've had the pleasure of sending off two employees with between 15-30 years of service in a way they will remember, and we should show them that by making a lasting impression for their next journey. We need to create a walk through memory lane as a way of giving back.

After being notified of their retirement, here are a few things we should do:

Pictures of Them in Their Element

In the past, I have sent off retiring employees by capturing them in their element:

- During their last few days, get photos of them working
- Get pictures of them in front of their building
- Get pictures of them with your group as a team photo
- Find some old pictures of them over their tenure
- Make some funny pictures using photo editing software and insert their photo into interesting back drops.

Get Feedback from Your Department and Other Areas

Inform your team of the news, but tell them to keep it quiet. Ask them to tell a story about how they remember agent X. This personalized story will be included in a PowerPoint deck with their name next to the story. Don't just include your department, but also others areas the employee may have interfaced with and engaged with those individuals, and have them tell a story. You'll be surprised on what you get and at the end of the day; it's a nice touch. Include some examples into the deck.

This is an example of something, I wrote for an employee that was retiring from my team in 2013.

Joe McGee, RA Manager of Tech Support

In July 2013, I took Agent White to Hackensack, NJ and it was a hot day 85-90 degrees. We took my vehicle and my A/C wasn't working for the 2 hour drive down and back. Agent White was instrumental in helping fix the product so it could run tests once again. That night Agent White took a cold shower and probably was on the verge of heat exhaustion. To this day Agent White always jokes with me for that hot day and frequently leaves me coupons for Pep Boys to get my AC fixed.

Put This into a PowerPoint Presentation

Put all of this into a PowerPoint presentation about their journey through the company. Also, have some fun with it by doing trivia questions and relate it to relevant movies or songs.

For example: Agent White started in the same year this movie was released, and list the date and movie.

Poster Board

Get a nice-sized posted board and hang it up on the floor of your department. Ask your co-workers to sign it, as well as people from any other areas that interfaced with that employee. This will be provided to the employee before they leave.

Give Them the Presentation and Display It

If your department has a T.V. screen, put them to use by presenting the retirement deck for the day.

Be sure to give the employee the deck for them to take home and print out. I would also recommend e-mailing the deck to the employee, for them to have the file electronically.

Send Off the Right Way

During their last day, contact the employee's family and as a surprise. Invite them to come to work and join in the celebration meal that the management team will provide.

Having family close by is a nice touch, and their family can understand the environment where they have spent so much time; thinking of it as their second home.

18. Remember Me Through Creativity

My daughter found herself with a new teacher and ultimately, new classmates for first grade. She wanted to stand out among her classmates—to be remembered. But how? One of the things she does well is helping others with work assignments. To be remembered, she would do this consistently throughout the year. At the end, she was recognized as the superstar of the classroom in an auditorium setting.

This is much like what we need to do as leaders and individual contributors; we must stand out among the crowd to be remembered. This all starts at the beginning.

Individual Contributor Interview

In what ways are hiring managers looking for their perfect match? It's quite simple: you will either stand out as being remembered in the interview, or you will not. One of the things I don't see often, but would hope to one day, is for interviewees to break out of the traditional presentation of their resume. How often do resumes look the same? How often am I drowning in word after word? This is the traditional sense candidates are presenting themselves in. Instead, these top five creativity selling points should give you the proper foot in the interview before even opening your mouth. Let's look at five different things to make you stand out among the group:

1. The resume should pop. Think about the companies you worked for in the past. We should add company logos to make the resume stand out
2. Present your resume in a timeline format by year.
3. Make your resume interactive; put it in a label for a water bottle or candy bar. Great conversation point and you are being creative.
4. Let's face it: in this day and age, it's all about technology. Make a video at your current employer setting, with approval of course. Talk to various co-workers and managers about things you did to improve your role, etc. Make titles of the people talking along with their phone numbers.
5. Put your skills on paper in a pie chart and include QRC scanner codes to bring them to *LinkedIn* pages or other pages.

Hiring Managers: Finding the Right Candidate

Finding the right individual for your team is much like house hunting; it's a process in which you are qualifying them against your must-haves and ranking them against others.

In what ways should you find the right person? This process will take time, but it's important you have a process in place to enable you to find that person. Are you doing the things below?

1. Employment Assessment- Match the interviewees' current skill set against your skill core competencies.
2. Allow your employees to attend the interview, give their opinions, and ask their own questions. After all, they are the front line staff and may have a different perspective.
3. If it's a troubleshooting position, put them on the spot. Have a mock up and says it's broken, and see how they would approach fixing it.

Ensure the Employee Wants It

From the start of the interview, it's up to you to ensure this is a fit for them, and if it's not, then don't keep going and waste time. It's time to accelerate the interview. One particular candidate told me he didn't really like call centers, and this position was for a call center. I told him to think of a time when he was going to purchase a new vehicle.

A sales member asked if you were definitely sold on this brand. You told him "No, I'm looking at other brands." A smart sales team member would not give me a price, as he may be fishing. "To get your best price, come back when you're sold on the brand, and I'll get you the best price." This is no different.

Towards the end of the interview, when you ask the candidate questions, what kind of questions are they asking? Are they very interested in the position, or are they fishing for other opportunities? You are able to tell based on their questions and eagerness for the job.

After a day of interviewing, I have narrowed it down to two candidates. But how do I decide when there is only one position open?

Bring both employees back and have them sit for 2-3 hours with the existing staff, and see how well they are perceived by the current staff. Give them a greeting and just simply put them on the phone.

This bold move is needed to see who catches on the quickest and ultimately, is not afraid of being under pressure. I have done this in the past and it has allowed me to make a decision quicker than overlooking them by my notes. This final test will show you who the right candidate is for the job.

19. Live For Tomorrow Not Today

Have you ever walked in a house built in the 1800s-1900s and wondered about the history that transpired in this property? Imagine that these doors and the walls have heard more conversations throughout their time and are very wise through their tenure. Wouldn't it be interesting to have a recording of all of the conversations this property had heard over time?

If we bought the property today and lived there, our legacy would be built and engraved into its history. It's about how our story shapes tomorrow and the future.

Just imagine if you could see how many hands have turned the door knobs on the property.

As leaders, we also need to be sure we paint our road map and live for tomorrow and not today.

Five Year Mark

During your time in your management role, think of these between the first year and fifth year.

1. Improve the role from where it was the previous year.
2. Ensure you are involved in at least two projects in addition to your regular work. Challenge yourself in a new project and set a timetable.
3. By the fifth year, start looking at where you want to go with your career.

What Are You Doing For You

More times than we can count, we, as managers, are always concerned about the development of our employees, but are not focused on our own development.

You, as a manager—are you thinking about yourself and formulating a plan to stay current with your development? The answer is that this is sometimes forgotten. I would consider getting involved in formal and informal training activities to stay current.

Formal

Let's face it: if you are a technology manager, are you also getting the proper training to understand the technology you are supporting as a manager?

Is there any certificate training that supports your call center, so that you can run your center correctly and efficiently?

1. PMP
2. ITIL
3. Six Sigma
4. Microsoft
5. CompTIA
6. HDI
7. And the list can go on.

Informal

Other ways to stay abreast of new technology to help you shape your understanding of the subject matter can be done informally:

1. Attending conferences
2. Attending offsite meetings with speakers on new technology workshops
3. Attending offsite meetings, such as: HDI with networking with other individuals and speakers

4. Internal or external technology meetings or webinars

As managers, we are consistently evaluating our team, but the bigger question is: what if, for the day, I were to do their job? Do you think you could do it, effectively? If the answer is no, you would fail miserably; then something needs to be done.

If you don't understand their skill level, then go through their training to get a better grasp of their view point. We should be able to comfortably fit into their shoes as their manager.

20. Break Through the Wall Don't Go Around It

Many times, in a support center, troubleshooting an issue may not go the way we often predict it should. In fact, it could even create more problems than the initial reported problem.

When an employee is able to break through to the other side and conquer the issue, this is something we should all praise and talk about.

Command and Conquer

Often times in a tier support center, we try to climb around the wall, or we stop at the wall instead of breaking through the wall. As managers, we know our support staff's knowledge and track record of what they do when they encounter an issue that's foreign to them. Let's take a quick look at the different call troubleshooting personalities:

Give It to Me

This personality does not care if they aren't familiar with the issue; they have the knowledge and tenure to research it and figure it out. They aren't afraid of new issues and, in fact, they want the challenge and they want you to give them the call. This is a great personality, but by doing so, and giving them the call, we should not forget about the employee who sent it to them. If you're doing this model and getting it to the "GIVE IT TO ME" personality, we just get the employee who sent the call proper motivation.

As time allows, let the employee see how this employee who is also in the same situation handles it. They don't know it, but they want it. Have that employee observe why they want it, and how they command and conquer that call. We need to change that employee's outlook, instead of just escalating it, because it's not the normal calls they are accustomed to. We need to introduce risk into that employee's mindset.

Escalate

This employee is safe in the calls they take and, in fact, they don't want anything to do with calls that are foreign to them. These employees end up escalating it to the next level, instead of taking the issue head-on. These employees need to see what going outside their comfort feels like.

I suggest the following methods to review issues with them, so that they can improve on any training gaps:

1. Have them write down the ticket number they send up.
2. Review the resolution of that ticket. Did they not know it? Or maybe overlooked it?
3. Have them work with the agent who resolved it, to brush up their skill level.

If you are tracking FCR (First Call Resolution), you should be looking at levels below 60%. Take a look at their tickets, and at the ones they are moving up. Are they valid?

You also should look at repeat call-backs. Is the resolution justified and valid? Or are we giving them something without thought just to get a resolution?

Share the Experience

No matter what the personality type, we must challenge them every day to think about a breakthrough they've experienced from the previous day. Have them bring and print out the ticket, and talk about how they turned around the call and acquired a resolution.

In doing so, the conversations that can take place at an informal meeting on the floor can spark great conversations surrounding the way we handled the situation and turned it around.

I would challenge you to invoke this method with your employees, and to share everyone's conversation in real time.

Make It About You After They Share With You

After they share an experience with you, be sure you reverse shoes and also share an experience of how you also were able to breakthrough an issue. This will show them that you don't always have the answer, but you're also able to fight through adversity.

See Chapter 28: "In the Element" for my example of how I championed my breakthrough with courage and persistence.

21. Playing Baseball with a Basketball

My daughter often asks what the point of sports is, because she doesn't get it. Who decides what balls to use or the purpose of the game? My daughter recently played dodge ball at a birthday party. She didn't understand why the game was invented. You have to be angry to throw balls at each other.

Many games such as: baseball have changed and evolved over the years.

I told my daughter if you tried playing baseball with a basketball, it wouldn't work out too well. The game and ball type have been chosen correctly for the type of game.

Let's look at history for a moment—surrounding the baseball. The 1925 ball was larger in size, weighed more, and gave the pitcher much less control in that the seam of the ball, which is much smoother and the thread is almost completely countersunk, so as to be flush with the leather of the seam.

In 1958, almost 25 years after Major League Baseball first made the specifications of its baseballs public, J.E. McMahon of The New York Times sought to update the public on the contemporary composition of a major-league baseball.

Major league baseballs start with a core of cork mixed with a small amount of rubber. This is covered by a layer of black rubber, then by a layer of red rubber. It is then ready for the winding process, where yarn is added to the core. This is done on a revolving machine—in a humid and temperature-controlled room.

As you can see, the years' subtle changes have been made to the sport of baseball—but not many. Think about your front-line staff for a minute, in the way they follow the posted procedures. If they are finding a better way that works for them, are they doing it or checking with management to present their idea? If they are doing it because they think it's better, it's time to talk to these individuals sooner than later.

Finding Better Ways

One of the most important factors for finding better ways should lie on the hands of the employee. This can be done by simply asking your front-line staff for ideas on how to improve the productivity and effectiveness of their daily work.

By asking, you will find varied items that the staff will pitch to you for ideas that could help them. It's important that they know they need to pitch these ideas and they do not simply just do them. The staff needs to be consistent among all agents.

Turn Errors into Learning Opportunities

Let's look at Herman Long who played baseball from 1889-1904. Herman Long managed to commit 1,096 errors while playing just 1,875 games. It's an average of more than one error every other day.

Look at your current staff right now. Are they making more than one error every day? What about your veterans? We need to turn these mistakes into learning opportunities. Our staff needs to operate like a well-oiled flawless machine and if they do not, we need to coach them immediately.

Coaching the Right Way

If you follow baseball, you will notice the base runner coaches that assist the base runner in making decisions.

Look at first base coaches. These are the guys who first bump the batter on the behind for reaching first base. He also keeps an eye on the pitcher, in case of a pickoff attempt. In baseball's information age, first base coaches are a way to gain an edge.

A good first base coach has a stopwatch in hand and a small black book in the back pocket of his uniform pants. When a batter reaches first, he times how long it takes the pitcher to release the ball after he breaks his hands during his delivery. The information is then provided to the runner.

This system has worked for many teams, and the factual information is used to obtain an advantage over the other team by using this data to arrive at a decision.

Coaching your team should be done strategically in the same manner. It should not come from a well-crafted e-mail explaining the issue.

You need to sit with your team and explain the effects of their mistakes and how it reflects on the bigger picture. If the agent is to fully understand the mistake and how important it is to be flawless, sitting with them is more effective than sending an e-mail and telling them to fix their mistake.

I Want To Hit a Home Run

During coaching sessions, the agents who show initiative and are consistently better than the expectations still want more. They often ask, "What can I do to be even better?" These are the agents who want to hit the home run. You, as their manager, need to paint the line and commit mutually to get the agent to the high expectations they instill in themselves.

Like many baseball stars, the key to hitting a home run is practice and technique. If your agent is not committed fully to the scope of your department, then they will never hit that home run.

Think about your team and what's holding them back from performing at their optimum level. This is the Kryptonite you must break, so that they can get to that high level.

Training Comes From Multiple Directions — Engross Yourself in These Words of Wisdom. Don't Throw It Away

In baseball, coaching comes from many different hats from the ball club. You have your general manager, batting coach, running coaches, mentors, etc. The biggest mistake is to turn a blind eye to the feedback provided to you. You probably have heard the expression, "You never know who your boss will be."

Here's an example of turning a blind eye to one of your coaches. In 2006, I worked as a Technical Trainer for a call center and ran into a situation regarding someone who wanted to turn a blind eye, just because I was just the 'trainer' and not the boss or general manager.

As the trainer, I would provide coaching feedback to every employee. I arrived at one of the employee's desks and coached him on troubleshooting. I wanted to know the reason was that called for the replacement of a board first without checking wires/voltage for any power issue. His answer was not verbal.

How did they interpret the importance of the training? The agent informed me he would put the paper in his filing cabinet, and I watched him drop it in his trash can. It was obvious this person didn't want to hear any feedback from me. Why? Because I was just a 'trainer'?

A few years later, when I was in a management role, I ended up taking him under my wing, and I found it appropriate to bring the conversation up. The moral of this story is to always understand that multiple people can be your coach, and that their feedback should be valuable and not a joke. You never know who your boss will be one day.

Sliding Head First Can Be Disastrous

Have you ever watched a slide into the base coming full-steam ahead, and head-first in baseball? It can be disastrous and dangerous.

We need to educate our first line of defense to properly respond to e-mails in a professional manner, and to not respond to your emotions. In my career, I have seen a lot of animosity between first level and second level support. It was always a pointing contest about what was done wrong. This responding to emotion can be disastrous.

If your teams are split up between managers and support levels, what you need to do to gain that trust and winning spirit is to involve each other.

Bring someone from tier two personnel, have them speak to tier one in a group setting, and give them some ideas about what they are doing well and what they can improve on. This same concept should be reversed for tier one speaking to tier two on ways communication can be more fluid, and feedback is always welcomed. Doing these things is a recipe for a winning department.

22. Being a Technical Detective Without a Badge

Just like many schools, a student's behavior and many other factors are evaluated to ensure that they are measuring for their grade levels. For example: my daughter is very proud that she makes 'gold' almost every day. Meaning, she followed the rules and helped others without being talked to.

As leaders, we must ensure our staff is also measuring up to the standards put in place for a successful contributor. It's up to us to ensure that we steer the ship correctly and consistently every day.

Are you, as a leader, taking the necessary time to be with your employee daily, not just weekly or monthly? Even having an informal discussion with them about anything shows you are taking time out of your day to be with them.

What is your employee's mission statement? Ask them the next time you sit with them. What I mean by this is: "Why do you come to work every day?" and "What are you looking to accomplish?"

We, as front line staff, control the direction of the call. A few things the employee must do are crucial for success, and this can be measured by properly managing employees through coaching and call evaluations.

An employee needs to have a vision of where they are going early on in the call. If they are spinning their wheels, then they should no longer guess on something they are unsure about.

What route should I take during the call? Often times, the biggest mistake made is wasting time with a bad decision. The employee needs to plan and decide sooner or later. What is the employee's vision for where the call is going? They need to have a plan and to execute this plan.

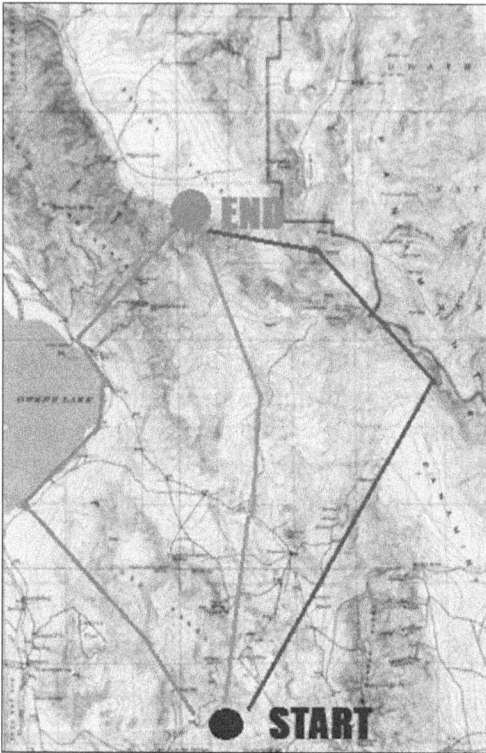

A call is much like a map with many different directions we can go.

For example: in the map above, you may notice a few choices you can choose in order to reach the 'end point.'

1. The first line is a wooded area; then follow a clear path near a lake with minimum dense mountains until the end.
2. The middle line is a straight shot up rough mountain terrain.

3. The last line is through a forest with access roads, before hitting an unknown mountain terrain towards the end.

If you were to use this map as an example, and if you ask your team what route they would take and why, you would see varied results.

Having all of the facts should influence the safest and most logical decision. While you are sitting, or performing a call audit with your team, what are you noticing from their handling of the call? Are they coming up with a plan closer to a resolution? Or are they taking the long route to disaster?

The key to see where they are going is to be with them throughout the journey part of the day. Let them know how they are doing, and if they are taking the long route to disaster, it's time to coach. An employee who knows the right questions to ask will result in a varied direction given by using the right probing questions.

On the next page, we will look at a map. In this example, if I was driving a car, I would have two options to arrive at my destination.

The two lines seem pretty close regarding what is faster. However, the upper route is 1.3 miles with a 4-minute arrival. The lower route is 1.4 mile with a 6-minute arrival. The upper route is the faster choice. Making the right directions can change, just like an agent's recommendation may change based on factual data and asking the right probing questions.

Asking the right probing questions is the key in factoring down the right direction to go in.

Probing Questions (The Right Way)

Let's say my corporate environment uses corporate blackberry handheld devices.

You receive a call in which the caller isn't getting any e-mail from their handheld device. A few questions should be asked in this scenario before the troubleshooting questions should begin. Here is an example of the right way:

1. Is this a new device? Answer: Yes
2. Did you submit the device for activation once receiving it? Answer: No.
3. The advisor can then gather information to ensure it's activated correctly.

Probing Questions (The Wrong Way)

Again, let's say my corporate environment uses corporate blackberry handheld devices. You receive a call in which the caller isn't getting any e-mails from your handheld device. A few wrong questions are asked, and your road to resolution is skewed.

1. Is your radio OFF due to the low battery or bad signal? Look top right hand corner. Answer: It's on.
2. Can you check your SYNCH options to ensure SYNCH is set to ON from the device? Answer: This is a new device, and it's on.
3. If this is a new device, did you submit for activation once receiving the device? Answer: No.

4. The advisor can then gather information to ensure it's activated correctly.

As you can see in this example, we wasted a few unnecessary questions by not asking the right questions from the beginning.

Much like our example above about the Blackberry Enterprise Server, our factoring can lead us in different directions by asking the right questions and using the logical probing questions before proceeding. We must have a plan of where we are going from the start.

Now, much like our map, the factoring of our decisions should influence the right path. Let's review another factoring decision that we need to make using the same map.

Let's assume that our start and finish positions have not changed, but instead of driving, we are now walking.

The best approach by walking—instead of driving—is right up the middle through the woods. This is shown by going up the middle in the map above. We shouldn't follow the same path as though we are driving. Your factoring decision should change by looking at the best option at all times.

This map has a significant meaning, as my challenge was walking or riding a bike to my friend's house. I soon realized the importance of changing the factoring of a decision is based on travel, and I did, in fact, use the 'woods' to arrive to my destination faster. By using the woods, I saved a significant amount of time by factoring all the options.

This same approach is needed by your front-line staff to approach the situation by asking the right questions.

Applying the Approach in Your Team's Dialogue

It's all about the approach. I learned from my daughter that in order to get what you want, you need to understand who you're dealing with: your audience.

It's about the approach and if said that right, their eyes light up like a Christmas tree. This understanding applies to all logical conversation. I told her today to "pick up her cup." She said "No."

I said, "Give me your cup." She picked it up and handed it me. Or think of it this way: if your child needs to clean your room and you tell them to do so, I bet it will not get done.

Instead, try the approach of asking for them to be 'your helper', and start emphasizing the word 'helper.' If they know they are important, they are more inclined to help you, but in the end, they are accomplishing the main goal of cleaning the room. This same train of thought should be applied to your teams.

23. Leading the Pack Should Not Be Ignored

Often times, recognition should be occurring in most schools; especially in growing minds. One of the things that my daughter's school does very well is the 'Friday Phone Call.'

On Fridays, they select an individual—someone that helped others throughout the week and exhibited leadership qualities—and turn it into a recognition phone call. This is done by calling the parent from the class with the child's participation, by using a speaker phone and informing the parent why they were selected.

I feel that without this type of program, the kids who are mentoring others would not be recognized for their efforts. This also applies in your department.

One of the biggest misconceptions is the 'leader vs. manager functions.' You don't have to be in management to be exhibit leadership qualities. Let's take a look at the differences of both manager and leaders:

Leaders

- Mentor
- The Example of Success
- Inspire Others
- Understand the Bigger Picture
- Coach
- Own Tasks

Managers

- Develop Talent
- Solve Operational Puzzles
- Set The Tone and Mission Statement
- Plan
- Delegate Tasks

If you look around at your current team, I'm sure you will find a leader who is inspiring and mentoring your team right now.

These qualities found in your leaders should not be ignored. They are operating at optimal levels, but may want more.

Once these individuals have been targeted, are you sitting down with them and setting a career path? These are the folks who, in no better way of saying it, are bored. Don't wait.

Have that conversation today, so that they can do more with their talent and do not consider leaving the company.

The next time you are thinking about these individuals, think of them as your alphas—like with wolves.

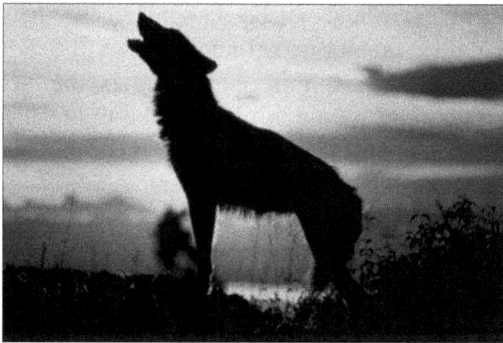

Wolves live and hunt together in groups called 'packs.' A wolf pack is really just another name for a family of wolves. A pack is usually made up of an adult male wolf, adult female wolf, and their offsprings. Pack sizes range from three to twenty wolves. The pack leaders are the alpha male and female. These two animals are dominant over all the other wolves in the pack. The alpha male and female are the only wolves that breed and produce an offspring, and they also get to eat first at kills.

Alpha

The Alpha Wolf's responsibilities are to carry out the following functions:

- Maintain order
- Make decisions
- Be alert for change

Think of the alphas as someone who will be able to fill your role as manager one day. The alpha employee can be trusted, such as with a project you can delegate to them. Make them in charge for one day, and the other employees will know how valuable they are for that responsibility. Even more so, the employee will know the value they have earned overtime from being under your wing.

24. Paddling with Broken Oars in Piranha-Infested Waters

One of the passions my daughter is interested in is drawing and creating art. More often than not, she is in need of new crafty construction paper, or perhaps she simply needs new tools to make the piece into a masterpiece.

Let's think about that for a moment: the tools are needed not just to get the job done once, but to get the job done many times efficiently and correctly. If we don't have the proper tools in place, let's face it, we might as well be paddling with broken oars in piranha-infested waters.

I want you to really think about your organization and the tools used to help support the problems you are faced with daily. What kind of tools or labs are in place to replicate their issues in-house?

For example: if you are supporting a lot of remote users using preconfigured routers, or perhaps preconfigured thin clients, how are your employees getting the proper training on these calls? Is it just merely looking at documents and manuals? In this example, it would be beneficial that the organization get an exact setup, so that the technical support staff can properly review the equipment and handle accordingly.

No matter what the rollout is in your organization, it's a proven fact that a picture is worth a thousand words. But what is an exact replica worth? I'll tell you that this replica will help your team through the training and understanding of the technology. If you're thinking about running a budget on new projects, and have not considered doing a mock replica of a setup, you should move on this initiative, immediately.

Start taking a look at the technology that you're interfaced with, by running a department. Do you have the proper tools in place to run an efficient operation? What I mean by this is: from the very basic to the most complex solutions, all should be looked at. Simple things like a chair falling apart or not having a proper plan for when the power goes out are very important things.

When was the last time you reviewed your disaster recovery plan? When was the last time you reviewed the procedures to field incoming calls when your ITSM tool goes down? Or simply when the power goes off—what is your contingency plan?

When an outage occurs, do you have the proper tools to identify and detect the root cause of why this occurred? In many corporations, this is crucial, so that the same mistakes—whether driven by the system, human, or other—can be prevented. This is why a proper change and release team and process should be established in all corporate environments.

One of the last things that would scare me being on a boat with broken oars in piranha-infested waters would be: the lack of preparation. Think about how your employees are engaged in new company values. Do they know them when they are put on the spot? If the employee was given the proper tool before heading out, this would have been prevented.

The last thing you would want is: a high-level executive doing spot checks on your employees, only to find out your department does not know them.

Whose shoes does that fall on? The answer is to look down: it's on you.

25. Influencing Change Through Storytelling

It's that time of year again, when our children start school for their first day with their new teacher. For my daughter, who is entering the second grade in September 2016, this can be a scary moment for change.

In fact, when we were informed of the announcement about her new teacher, she was disappointed. Keep in mind, she had never met the new teacher before, but had her mind set on who she wanted. There is always caution in not giving someone a chance or being set on your ways without knowing them first. Never judge someone without knowing them or hearing their story. I told my daughter a story about judging people, and for her to give her new teacher a chance.

One day, a father and son were on a train ride through the country with beautiful trees and passing clouds visible through the windows. During the ride, the man's son was noticing that the trees they were passing were now behind him. He then said, "Look at the clouds; they are following us." A young couple noticed the boy's comments and approached the father. The young couple said, "Is there something wrong with your son? He should see a doctor!"

The man said, "We just got back from the hospital after the surgery for my son." He said, "You see, my son was born blind, and he's seeing them for the first time."

Especially with call centers, things can change like the wind, and how we present change can be challenging.

Think about the next time you need to change a KPI, and explain it to your team. How do you approach it? There are a few key factors on how we should present change and in doing, so will allow you to have the upper hand in influencing the change to your team. Follow these five steps for a successful delivery:

Step 1: Why Are We Doing It? Tell a Story in Doing So

With change, we must explain the reasons why the change is valid. Why we are doing it—with the benefit and the bigger picture, so that they fully understand the extent of the change and how it applies to them.

For example: recently, we implemented a change regarding the ASA (Average Speed of Answer). Based on feedback, it was evident that we needed to improve it 60% faster than we were currently doing it.

In my sales pitch to the team, explaining the 'why' is much like selling something, so that they can see the value of it. I informed the team that right now, we are currently recognized by JD Power's as one of the top-rated tech support departments of our industry. In order to stay competitive and keep this high level of support, we must make changes that are aligned to the service our competitors are providing.

Think about what consumers want. When you buy anything, whether it is a car or a snow blower, you want to know the service behind the manufacture. How is rated? How is it perceived? These factors are crucial for a decision to be made. Not doing these changes that would put us at a serious disadvantage. This would put us behind everyone else. This would mean loss of sales and ultimately less calls for our technical support staff.

In order to bind the pieces together, simply tell a story to show them the value in all they do and why the change must be done.

We all have a story we can relate to—bring the change into something that pulls it all together. Find the story that relates to the change and start using the story immediately to drive the point home.

Step 2: Show Me the Data

Like anything else, factual data also tells a story. With any big change, we must show them the data and how it supports the change. This should be done in a graphical form, which is easy to follow; a visual aid always tells a better story in a graphical form.

By showing your team the factual data, you are giving them no excuse for why your change cannot be done.

Step 3: Get a Cheerleader

One of the important factors you probably already know is that: word travels fast. In the matter of change, whether good or bad, people will talk openly on how they feel about it. This word will travel fast among the floor and soon, people may be influenced by other co-workers before making their own opinion. Why? It's simple. They trust the high performer's opinion on the topic at hand.

If that high performer is not on board, then the whole team could feel the same way. The best thing is to know the cheerleaders in your department. Who are the trusted resources your co-workers trust? We must ensure these cheerleaders truly believe in the change, so that no negative opinions are formed.

Step 4: Set the Expectation for Results

After delivering the change, we must set the expectation of when these changes start and when we will be able to monitor it for tracking. At the end of the monitoring stage, a few things will happen.

If the factual data supports the change, then there is no reason why the agents cannot give you what is expected.

The team comes close but falls short of the expectation

Worst-case scenario: the whole team is nowhere close to the goal. This could be a result of the unknown factors that caused the skewing of the goal. Time to go back to the drawing boards. This should only happen when poor planning or unknown factors influenced the failure of the change.

Step 5: Remind Them of Their Achievement

Once a successful change was defeated, we must remind them of what they accomplished. This is very important, especially when new change comes on the radar. We can use this as 'fuel for the fire.' Remember that time we presented the change on XYZ? We defeated that change; this is no different. Your team must feel the accomplishments and not fear the next hurdles.

26. Having the Winning Spirit

Like many establishments, we want to retain our workers and for them to like what they do. My daughter asked me a very mature question. She simply asked, "Why do you go to work every day?" This is a funny question, because my perception of the answer has changed over the years. My answer to the questions prior to 2009 was to have fun and push myself every day. My answer after 2009—after the birth of my child—was different. My answer now is to make money to support my family, but also to challenge myself every day. It's funny that as we grow in our careers or in life; our outcome is much different.

According to research by the management-consulting firm Gallup, 71% of American workers are either not engaged or actively disengaged from their jobs; with highly educated and middle-aged workers the least likely to feel involved in and enthusiastic about their work.

As we learned in Chapter Three, the 'Learn It, Teach It, Apply It Principle' can be used to engage the employee creatively beyond this. What else can we do to set the atmosphere and really know that our workers want to come to work every day?

Like all departments, there will also be one or two individuals that bring bad vibes into the work place. This is how rumors start, and it can be disastrous for you to have these individuals bring their negative attitude to others. How do you get them to have that winning spirit?

It could be that these individuals are set in their ways and their attitude is a way of gaining attention, since they are not proving themselves at optimal levels. This is their way of creating an illusion to get attention from anybody willing to believe in them. This is much like what a rattlesnake can do when they want attention. To show they feel threatened, they use their rattle. The rattlesnake will make noises with their tail, and it is a sound of—possibly—balls moving back and forth from the friction of moving. This is probably how the idea of the baby rattle was conceived for bringing attention to others.

What if I told you that if we were to cut the rattlesnake's tail open, you would find no balls that are making the noise? This was an illusion, if you will, or more precisely, merely a small object inside that was vibrating to cause the noise.

Now, let's go back to the employee without the winning spirit, and compare them to the rattle snake. Both the snake and the employee are in their element where they are allowed to use this illusion to their advantage. The key for them to change is to take them out of their element and to areas they are not comfortable in, or areas that are new to them.

For example: if we were to take that rattlesnake and put it in the Atlantic Ocean, how do you think it will do? How many times will it use the rattle effectively? The resolution is quite simple. Move the employee outside of their normal routine and have them start asking themselves questions to prove that their value is still relevant and important.

Give Them Marching Orders; Make Them Valuable

Tell them: "Great news! I have selected you for a very important project, as your feedback is very valuable to me." Have them do a project or a write up on an idea of how to improve productivity for front line staff, or on anything you see fitting for their development.

This unexpected news would seem fitting for your best employee. However, we need to engage even those who are not actively involved, and make them feel involved.

Have Them Sit with You for the Day

By having them evaluate you for the day, they may better understand all of the things that go on behind the curtain. Allow the employee to be with you for the day, and understand the things that the management is involved in and how it relates to them.

This also allows them to see that you're an authentic leader and are willing to allow them to join you for the day to take their mind off their normal routine.

Off-Site Networking or Lunch Meetings

During the month, I would advise an off-site lunch meeting for the employee to get them away from the office setting for a while; which puts their mind at ease from the typical meeting setting. The other thing I would advise is to involve them in any off-site networking meetings with you, so that they can network with other individuals and companies. This is a huge advantage in molding their growth and development, by getting away and meeting different people.

27. Chair of God

How many of us would daydream when we were kids? How many of us would play with action figures and dolls and make up a story? Sometimes, in the work world, we as employees need to create an atmosphere for a self-rewarding 'thank you.' We create this illusion to allow a break from redundant work. The only caution by doing this is the trouble that may follow.

My daughter is constantly creating stories while playing with her dolls and does so to keep her mind is engaged. As an individual contributor, we must also do the same.

Back in 2006, I worked for a call center as Level Two support, in which we had about four workers per cube area. One particular day, my very good friend Heath Hunt and I were competing in the tickets we handled and we wanted some way to showcase that we were, in fact, showing great strides in our daily workflow. But how?

In the lobby of our building, we noticed an old massage chair that seemingly was being used as an extra seat but didn't appear to work. On that particular day, we dragged the chair down the hallway.

We set up the chair in the center of the four-person cube and decided to give it a purpose. It was decided that we would use this chair for a morale booster and for us on a thriving day of success; the person who exhibited the best work would be able to use the chair.

We also had wireless headsets, and throughout the next few days, we took turns using the chair while we were on calls and reclined with our feet up. This was our informal pat on the back for the hard work. We decided to use this chair as the 'control,' for illustrating that, and included it in our everyday routine.

The next day or so, after our neighboring department had noticed that we were more than comfortable taking calls with our feet up, they made an inquiry to our boss.

Of course, it didn't take too long for word to spread and for people to talk about what we were doing.

We received a group chat invitation from our boss

Boss: I hear that there is a new addition to your cube?

Joe McGee: The Chair of God?

Heath Hunt: Yes

Boss: Where did it come from?

Heath Hunt: Around the Corner.

Boss: Go put it back where it came from.

I branded this type of reward as the '*Chair of God*,' as I think in many ways, that's exactly what it felt like sitting in this chair. We had conquered a great task and we needed to sit on our throne for a moment.

We created this illusion to keep up the winning spirit of our competitive natures. This type of ice breaker is needed for an individual contributor, but of course, you should follow the rules and not touch furniture.

This type of action from us was exhibited because like many technical positions, it's a thankless job. We needed that extra bit of 'living in that moment.' We needed to be the superhero for the day, and this was the way we were going to showcase that moment.

A few days of an ice-breaker is always needed to ensure a non-redundant environment. I would challenge you to find that extra spark in your environment and make your team challenging, but of course, the moral of the story is to always ask the boss before you act among yourselves.

28. Being in the Element (Showing Your Value)

How many times on the radio do you hear your jam song? You've been waiting all day for that song, and now, you are in your element or groove.

My daughter has certain songs that she likes to dance to, and often wants to listen to these songs, while she is drawing or painting. We all have these songs in their back of our minds.

I'm going to tell you a story about being in the element, and how to leave a lasting impression even after you leave that role. The secret ingredient is to make it your own—, to figure it out and take ownership of it.

In 2009, I worked for Desktop Support and supported many different departments' computer needs for internal employees within three different buildings. The support structure was broken up by desktop support, and the application support for home-grown applications built by their respective teams.

One particular application was failing to launch to authenticate the user correctly for one particular user in another state. This application used Oracle SQL Database Client and specific server paths to connect to the database front end. The ticket had bounced around from the application support team, and was now back to desktop support. This application was new to me and I had not previously interfaced with it.

After doing my typical research, which included prior tickets and knowledge base searches, I was not finding concrete answers. I then approached the application team to give me an overview of how the application worked, and to see a working client in action. I needed to know how it connected and what prerequisites were needed in order for a successful connection.

I then had access to a working version and started to keep track of how the application worked, and reviewed the files needed to connect. I found that it was possible that a certain .INI file had been corrupt and/or was missing. I also found that the network share that the Oracle files were pointed to was not connected on his end.

After working vigorously for a day or so, I figured it out and documented my results in the ticket. As time went on, more and more issues surfaced and other desktop techs were not having much success in resolving the issues.

By this this time, I had become the un-official SME (Subject Matter Expert), because I stuck with the issue and made it my own.

As I continued through the journey of helping solve these issues, I also created a troubleshooting guide on what kind of issues could arise and provided the detailed fixes for each one.

Once this document had been worked on and revised, I sent it to other desktop techs in other states that also interfaced with this system, along with the local support and application support. When it came time to re-package the install file, I was included to make that happen by providing the package team with the necessary files and workflow of the application.

Now, let's step back for a second and review what just happened with me as a desktop technician. I took an issue that I knew absolutely nothing about, and I did what? I owned the issue and showed my value of maintaining the patience to resolve it. I became an SME and a trusted source to help the application team and other desktop technicians to solve these issues.

Later in 2009, I ended up moving to a manager role, but still stayed in close contact with the application team, even with a new role.

Whether you are an individual contributor or a manager, you must show the value in all you do. This is a perfect example of how to champion the issue and be proud of the outcome. I challenge all of you to apply the same courage and persistence to achieve success.

As we learned in Chapter Twenty about breakthroughs, we don't want to be the person who 'escalates' to only take issues they are comfortable with. We need to be the "Give it to Me" personality who wants the challenge and needs the challenge. Think about your workflow and if you are challenging yourself enough. If you're not being challenged, then give me a call and I'll put you up to the task of trying to resolve the issue first hand.

Fighting Through Change

To provide more context from Chapter 25: "Influencing Change through Storytelling," we need to fight through change and look at all the available options.

For example, in 2009, at our 24/7 call center, we were looking to increase our resolution goal by 5-10%. The first thing we had to look was the calls coming in, and if were they appropriate. What do I mean by that?

I started to realize that we had a large number of incidents for break/fix issues coming into the hotline that was more for request type calls rather than break/fix. These calls are not appropriate and reduce our potential for possible resolution. After discovering many different requests that were coming into the hotline, it was time to attack.

I put my ITSM tool to work and started to run some reports to show me what kind of tickets were simply asking for something and NOT a request. After I had identified these types of tickets, it was time to start contacting the appropriate line of business and engage them in changing the way these were handled. The key for acceptance is the approach.

When approaching these lines of business, you must remember: it's not about you—it's a mutual gain. You need to show them the benefit of switching their tickets into the platform that accepts requests. Sell them on the benefits of your ITSM tool's powerful options that are available to them.

This would include SLAs you can put into place for each ticket.

If you were to start meeting these lines of business—and it would just be about you—that conversation wouldn't go over too well in winning them over. As time went on, I was able to target multiple lines of business and start to have the initial conversation of what our hotline did, and how they could handle these requests better.

After all was said and done, I was able to deflect 200-500 tickets a month into a new system and we did, in fact, hit our new resolution goal. I was also recognized in a company town hall for my efforts for this reduction.

The key is to look at all opportunities to help you reduce a goal that was put in place. We shouldn't just expect a change without doing anything about it. As you can see through my experience, opportunities for improvement will always be there. You must start looking and identifying them to help with your goal.

29. Understanding Boundaries

In our society, we are surrounded by boundaries in more ways than you may realize or think about. We have town boundaries and state boundaries that outline the proper city or state lines. If you look at the simple task of going from point A to point B, we mostly drive a vehicle to accomplish reaching our destination.

If you look at this more closely, as we are driving, we are staying in lanes; boundaries that are set by town and state mandates. You may have employees tell you that they don't like the rules, or that they like to bend the rules. In this case, remind those employees that they are actually following the rules in everyday life. They are stopping at red lights. They stay in their lane on the highway and they don't drive in two lanes.

We, as a society, understand these mandates and uphold our duty as a citizen to maintain our vehicle in the proper lane as per the laws governing each municipality.

Whether you are an individual contributor or in a managerial role, we all must understand the chain of command that we work inside, and that it should be obeyed; much like staying in the correct lane while driving.

Even if you are doing something for the greater good of the department, the chain of command and scope of work should be followed. As an example of this: in 2008-2009, I was leading a team of agents by carrying out supervisor duties. I take pride in finding opportunities of holes and trying to fix them when the opportunity comes knocking. However, is it the right thing to do? By doing so, are you following the chain of command?

In my example, it's undeniable that I'm a very good with people and exhibit great leadership and manager attributes, or else I would not be recognized for what I have done or be where I am today.

In retrospect, in 2008-2009, my following up on an opportunity should have followed the chain of command and been given to my senior for them to carry out the task instead of me.

I didn't understand the chain of command, and was even told that, "I stepped outside the boundaries of the position." My initiative and eagerness on spearheading initiatives was not appropriate for my current title.

I should have delegated the tasks instead of handling them myself. I should have given what I had to management, and then waited for them to allow me to do it is how these events should have occurred.

However, today I'm a senior manager and doing the same type of work I was doing then. My talent was ignored and I was held back so someone else could have taken the credit for my work. I will ask you this: is that right or wrong? The answer is simple: it's not right or wrong. It's following the chain of command.

Understanding the Chain Of Command

It's important that you, as an individual contributor or manager, understand the reporting structure in your organization. For example, if you don't know now who your boss reports to, then you need to really understand the structure of your department.

As an example, it would be career suicide if I was a manager in my department, and instead of e-mailing my boss at the director level, I e-mailed the VP or CTO of the company. This is something that you should never do. It could hurt your career as you are bypassing the chain of command.

A good exercise that I practice is to show the individual contributor staff how our organizational umbrella is outlined from a reporting sense. This is a good idea, so that they understand the faces and titles of the operation they work for. What's even more important is that if these VPs or executives were to visit your location, would your staff know what they look like and what they do? They should. It's time to educate your staff so they have the information sooner than later.

You Know the Answer but You Can't

More often than not, our talent level with our staff is very high. We take the time to groom them for the next level, but they may already be aware of how to solve the problem. The problem is: they need to work in the boundaries of that role, which is X, Y, and Z. By doing anything else, they are not doing the job correctly. In order to move up, the agent needs to understand their function and wait for the time to apply and prove they have the necessary skill to do the next level job.

By doing this job now, they are not proving anything and are only stepping outside the boundaries of the expected duties they should be doing.

We all have agents that are ready for the next level, and are eager to take their new car for a test drive, but their license is suspended until they move up to the next role as per policy. This is something we need to coach our agents on and we must ensure they understand why this is bad.

Much like in my career, I was on the same boat at one point. I had the itch to do more when I was a level one support technician in 2006. I knew I could do more— but instead of doing more, I showed them the value in all I did and that I was ready to move up when the opportunity presented itself. I eventually did move up to level two, but it takes patience and really believing in you. Don't think about what you can do— just showing them your value will get the success you itch for in due time.

30. The Yes Man

As leaders, we must know that we cannot take the world on our shoulders 100% of the time. It's up to you as the leader to prioritize your work load and dictate the work you can handle.

In 2009, I was on the leadership team managing a group of fifteen or so employees. Often times, I would be given tasks and projects by the other managers. I was always the 'Yes Man.' No matter what it was, I would take it on and finish the task at hand. It was known by the rest of the leadership team that my word was my bond, and I would get it done no matter what was on my plate. I handled the workload well and set timetables and started prioritizing my work based on the timetables of the projects given to me.

At the time, I knew that these folks—whether it was other management or project managers from other departments—wanted to bring it to me because they trusted me to complete the task in a timely manner. I believe that over time, different people are flagged for different types of tasks, just because of past positive experiences. We should not always be the 'Yes Man'. We need to share the wealth of projects evenly among your subordinates.

It was later advised to me by other members of the management, that we are always pulled in many directions. Even though you are good at solving everyone's problems, a good leader needs to say "No," and to know when to delegate tasks and when to turn them away. This type of feedback was something that I was not expecting. In my eyes as a new leader at the time, I was doing more than what was expected. I was exceeding expectations because I was doing more.

That's a big mistake for new leaders. Don't always assume more is better.

Surprisingly, I was first shocked to be told to turn a blind eye and turn the projects away. Am I letting them down by not accepting? Will my reputation be tarnished by doing so?

After time, this type of thinking really stood out to me. My understanding of what being a complete leader means by definition came together. I'm really not the super hero, and I should not be expected to solve every problem all the time.

By sharing this experience, I want you, as a leader, to really start thinking about what I am saying. It's okay to say "no" and/or to delegate some of these tasks. Give it a try and you will be on the way to being even more effective as a leader by not taking on the world.

In 2012, when I was preparing to leave this company in my leadership role, one of the members of the management asked me to do something before I left. Of course, to throw salt on the wound, my response was "no."

Of course, I was joking. But the moral of the story is: that this type of feedback really changed my initial beliefs of leadership that doing more was needed to succeed in this role. I learned through this experience that that's not entirely true, and I have grown in leadership because of it.

In closing, I want you to think about how you are perceived as a leader by your team. I think the real testament would be to simply do a random survey and get honest feedback from your team. By doing so, are there any common themes people are seeing? Can they be changed for the better?

Another thing you can do is to do the same thing with other managers and find out how you are perceived by them. This will also open your eyes as a leader on items that could be changed for you to be more effective. I would recommend that if you are not doing these random feedback assessments with your direct reports and subordinates, you should start doing so.

You may think you are perceived in a certain positive way, but in reality, it's the opposite and is negative. You won't know until you start asking.

This feedback is valuable and we, as leaders, can make subtle changes to make us into a more polished leader.

31. Communicate like You're Talking to Your Significant Other

Many companies often struggle with lack of internal communications in their organizations. For example: a new change is being released into the environment. The release team is working with the change team on the proper timing and approval to release this change into the environment.

The problem is: nobody communicated this change to the internal service desk who might be receiving calls about this. It seems oftentimes, departments inside the same buildings don't talk to each other. We must communicate like we're talking to our significant other. Communication must always be clear and consistent at all times.

If you have children, you must know that getting them on and off the bus can be very demanding. We communicate with our significant other as to who will be getting them on and off each day. How do you think the relationship would go if we didn't communicate the bus schedule each day? Do you think our child would be happy being brought back to the school due to the lack of communication among their parents?

Much like a relationship, if communication is poor, then failure in that relationship is the likely outcome. In your everyday journey, we must have clear communication at all times. When I say at all times, I even mean the basics. For instance, when you, as a manager, go out of the office—whether for vacation, or travel—are you informing your team of this? If I told you some managers don't, would that surprise you? Communication should not be one-sided and needs to be mutually the same between you and your direct reports.

I would bet that if any company released a survey which asked for suggestions to improve yourself as an individual, I would bet that communication would be listed among the top things needed to improve.

Think about how your team is using communication throughout the day. Is it in the realm of expectations? For example: if I'm going to be out of the office on vacation, and I'm a phone advisor and I have a list of pressing issues, did I inform my manager they needed to be reassigned while I was on vacation?

You should also consider how you are perceived by your communication with your team. What kind of personality are they seeing among your work ethic? Or are you just were using chat and e-mail as your preferred method?

One of the bigger questions typically asked is: what percentage of communication is made up from the body language. The answer is actually 55%.

The figure 55% comes from research that Albert Mehrabian undertook in 1971; the results of which are still often quoted today. Mehrabian basically came to the conclusion that communication, on a face-to-face basis, is thought to consist of three separate elements:

- Words (what is actually said)
- Tone of voice (how we say the words)
- Body language

All three of these elements can be conveyed at the same time to express an overall message. Often, the tone of voice and body language are combined to become the most powerful form of communication. However, body language which forms a large part of non-verbal communication is often used on its own. The non-verbal is to be one of the most 'telling' modes of communication. Through his research, Mehrabian also surmised that proportionally, the three elements were not of equal importance. He claimed that in face-to-face communication, the majority of what is put across is portrayed as non-verbal communication.

This is why face to face communication is the most effective method of communication and should be utilized the most. With face-to-face communication, all three elements together words; body language, and tone blend together to drive the point home.

In his research, the three communication elements were broken out by percentage as shown below:

- Words (the literal meaning) account for 7% of the overall message
- Tone of voice accounts for 38% of the overall message
- Body language accounts for 55% of the overall message

Therefore, through face-to-face communication, the nonverbal communication part becomes the most powerful mode of communication that managers must take advantage of.

32. Document, Document, Document

My daughter is really into documenting what we are doing and where are we going, especially on vacation. The plan for the day should be well-documented, because my daughter loves to see what places we are going to in advance. This is much like managing and tracking your team's progress, which can be done in a simple way.

Whether you're a new leader or a veteran of the trade, one of the important things we should be doing is: to document, document, and document our employees' every day journey. This includes all of the good things, along with the suggestion for improvement you have provided to them throughout the year.

We should all be keeping employee folders for each of our direct reports, but the bigger question is: what's in these files? When it comes time to write up their performance review, what kind of specific examples do you have to highlight for the employee each year? Are you thinking on the fly? Or are you relying on your file for substance?

What works well for me is to keep a raw sheet for observations of the employee on any particular day. Just simply make a quick note on this paper, and you can refer back to it as needed. If you're not doing this it's going to be very hard to showcase an accurate depiction of the employee's progression. When I say a raw sheet, this is an example of what I mean:

Date: _____ Comment: _____
Date: _____ Comment: _____
Date: _____ Comment: _____
Date: _____ Comment: _____
Date: _____ Comment: _____

In these raw comments, you could have things as big or small as these examples. We can also see when it occurred, and how many patterns of this occurred whether position or negative.

Some examples below:

- Refused a call
- Stayed late
- Was not professional to co-worker or caller
- Picked up a shift for someone else
- Trained Agent White
- Written up for unprofessional behavior
- Submitted new ideas for call center improvement
- Caught in the wrong AUX Mode
- Never called out on this day

As you can see, these are simple things the employee is doing and can be crafted into the employee's performance review in the area it may fit.

You must not forget that the comments should not just be surrounded by 'negative' observations, but should also include 'positive' observations as well.

From a yearly perspective, these small comments will give you plenty of examples of how the employee operates and can easily build pros and cons based on this information.

The key is to use your employee folders and write this information into them in real time. This way, this information is fresh and not forgotten about; like if you had waited. Think about your current way of writing up a review. Are you only using your monthly numbers and comments as the main substance for your review?

Why not get some of these live observations documented? These should be a reminder of their perceived performance in real time. If you're not doing this now, I would start tracking your employee's observations on a daily basis.

33. Talking to Your Other self

My daughter, like many six year olds in school, will develop a close relationship and make a best friend. Whether on the bus or in class, a bond has been formed. My daughter met her friend and they soon shared thoughts of school and also made bracelets for each other. They helped each other in school when in need. This, in a way, is like looking at your own self in the mirror. You're making friends with someone that has similar interests and aspirations.

In my career from 2006-2009, I had the pleasure of having a conversation with my other self. His name was Heath Hunt.

I had first interfaced with Heath in 2006 when I was in a Trainer Role and he was in a Level Two support role. One day, Heath had stumbled into my training room to find out some of the things I was doing. From that day forward, we hit it off and became close friends. We started to form improvement initiatives together by him coming in and speaking to Level One on opportunities for improvement, as well as to highlight what they were doing very well. Over the next few years, we eventually left one company to be at the same company again. It was evident that we were both similar for many reasons, which allowed us to stay close in our work. Here is why:

- We were both work horses
- We both wanted more
- We both had goals of how we were going to do that
- We both respected each other's input
- We both have personal goals we are achieving outside of work

Especially in a support role in a corporate company, it's a must to have another self that has similar aspirations and goals of where they want to go. I found this in Heath Hunt, and I suggest you find your other self within your company. This other self is readily available for mentoring and helping with decisions, and/or talking through a decision.

I think the common disadvantage many employees are faced with is the lack of mentoring available. You can become immersed into a black hole of thoughtless hope.

For reasons such as: growth, development, and honest opinions, your other self is on the side-line with you to help you grow in these areas.

As your relationship continues, this bond of friendship and mentoring is so strong, that when you're guessing what direction to go in, your other self is beside you mentally with the answer. Have you ever been outside when Mother Nature blows a calm whispering wind that touches your neck so gracefully? That's a sign from your other self to do what you think is right.

I strongly believe that without each other's support and advice, both of us equally would not be as successful as we are today. Having these types of bounds are important and through the journey of your careers, it's a must.

Here is my other self below. Have you found your other self?

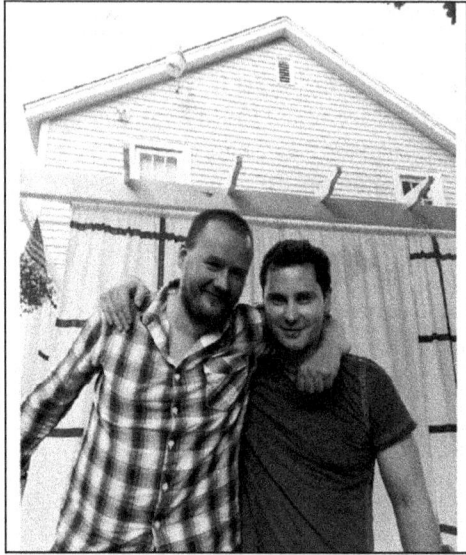

Left to Right: Joe McGee & Heath Hunt

34. Mountain Climbing with a Teleprompter

In most departments, we need to climb the highest mountain and soar to new heights and be proud of what the team did collectively that month. One of the many things that slip away is forgetting the milestones that were achieved by the team. How often do you ask yourself: "Gee, I know we did this initiative, but I don't recall when we implemented it?"

I bet that happens more often than you realize. So, the question is" how do we encapsulate this controlled content for viewing purposes down the road? We need to somehow go mountain climbing to soar to new heights, but by doing so, we need a teleprompter available to tell us what we did. I have the answer on how to better showcase your success stories.

In the past, newsletters have been very successful for showcasing your success. By showing this controlled content outlining your monthly initiatives, you're VPs and coworkers can remember the success stories each month. This encapsulation of success can be shared at monthly team meetings. Once the newsletter has been generated, we must get it out to the teams and VPs immediately. But how?

1. Start with an e-mail to the distribution list
2. Print off a hard copy and place it on each desk. Studies have suggested by putting a printed paper on one's desk, it will be read faster and more thoroughly than an e-mail.

What the e-mail allows you to do is: think of the initiatives and changes that took place that month. We then document and include pictures or changes that our department implemented, along with a respective date. This allows you as the manager to create controlled content on what you want the employee to remember.

One of the positive elements of the newsletter is when I need to refer to it when a change took place, but cannot find the exact date stated anywhere. Things like this should go in the newsletter, and they can then be found later. You can create the changes in real time and save the newsletter until it's complete and ready to send.

What Does the Employee Think?

Along with handing out the newsletter to the employee at a formal or informal greeting, we should also take it one step further with the sharing of information. As the group is gathered it's important to give them the floor and get feedback directly from them in real time.

Another thing we should do is to always respect the opinions of our direct reports. The best way is to simply ask.

During your next informal or formal meeting with the entire team, ask them as a group about what's on their minds, and go around the room. Ask them, "What do you want to talk about?" That's such an easy question to ask, and the beautiful thing about asking that question is the results that follow.

35. The Ten Keys to the Operating Manual (Summarization of a Successful Team)

As I mentioned at the beginning of the book, in leadership, there is no operational manual for running a successful team. In order to develop the keys to a successful department, a few factors should be in place:

- Emotion.
- Rules are rules.
- Push your team.
- Don't make a decision without considering all the factors and reviewing data.
- Don't assume until you ask questions
- A productive team must be properly motivated
- Make your employees want to come to work
- A thankless job should not be thankless
- Communicate with your team informally and formally
- Element of Surprise is a must

Key Number One: Emotion

Often in leadership, we let our emotion overcome and influence our decision. We forget that we are running a business and will often show favoritism among some employees. Your emotion should not overcome the right decision. Your direct reports are not your friends. They are there to help steer the business in new directions. The same applies to individual contributors: don't let it be personal when your co-worker gets a promotion over you. Don't let your emotion take over and list the reasons why you're better.

Key Number Two: Rules Are Rules

We, as managers, have put policies and procedures into place for a reason. When we discover something is not right with a rule that is being broken, we should be coaching.

The next thing we do is: to review and ensure they are then not making the same mistake again. We should not have the mentality, of: "Well, this policy is not severe—I'm going to give them a free pass." Everyone should be treated equally. If you aren't doing that now, then people will see right through your leadership style.

This same thought applies to your agents until a better way is presented. This is the way you should follow the rules. If you have a better idea, then be sure to present it.

Key Number Three: Push Your Team

Throughout the book, I have shown you many ways to push your team outside of their comfort zone. How many times do you think your team is bored at work? Why is that? The same redundant work is eating them alive and they want more. Using the LTA (Learn It, Teach It, and Apply It) principle will help them through their growth and development.

Key Number Four: Making Smart Changes

When the department needs to make a change to accommodate the line of business, we should not just simply throw a bunch of papers at the wall and hope it will paint a picture. We must review the data and then make the best decision based on the factual data.

Key Number Five: Ask Questions Before Coaching

How many times have you discovered a bad call? A call which maybe went in a different direction. Maybe a call where the agent was asking questions, but you couldn't understand why. When coaching the advisor, we must not just tell them they are wrong. We should instead ask them questions. Understand why they did what they did.

Key Number Six: Proper Motivation

Think about the team you manage. Are they properly motivated? Do they really want to push themselves and do more? What's their motivation to do more than just their job? The hardest part is to get someone who is satisfactory day in and out, to exceed or master at expectations. In our day and age, satisfactory is the new 'failed to meet expectations.'

Think about when you were in school and knew that selling X amount of cookies would get you the award at the end of day. Your employee must want to push themselves and if they do not, you need to develop a mechanism, so that they will in fact do their best work.

Key Number Seven: I Wake Up and Want To Come To Work

This is the message management needs to instill in their team. Your folks must be excited about coming to work every day and being happy in doing so. Think of the perks your employee is getting. Whatever that is, you must heighten the awareness of it, even at the initial interview level. If your average tenure for an employee's length of time at work is an average of 15 years, then use that as your selling point. Whatever the selling point is, ensure it stays that way and you'll be driving that message home, so that people want to come to work. The working environment needs to be fun and engaging. Is yours?

Key Number Eight: A Thankless Job Should Not Be Thankless

How many times does your salary employee stay late to handle calls? Well, that's them doing their job. The big challenge is to turn the daily experience into a fun experience. If an employee has gone above and beyond the new norm of expectations, then we should recognize them. Take the employee off-site for lunch. Give them a personalized note of the specific work they did and how it impacted the customer.

Let's talk about the personalized note and how that's replacing the thoughtless thank you card that was pre-printed and signed with machine ink. Some might think that's a nice touch with many organizations doing it, but with the same thousands or millions of cards that look the same, is it that personal?

I was surprised when my wife visited her bank and the very next day in the mail, she received a hand written personalized note from the teller in the mail. These are the kinds of things many different industry segments are trying—because it's a personalized note. This shows they took the time out of their day to acknowledge you. This is how our world is shifting into the less automated, redundant thoughtless card, and into the hand-crafted note. This is what will separate out the companies who care about your business and put others out of business.

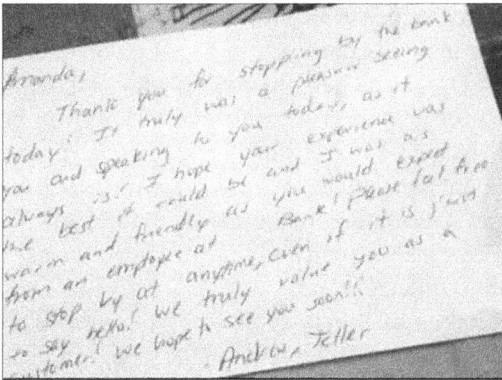

I'm going to make a prediction that more personalized notes will start to circulate between now and five years. If you have not received a personalized note yet, check your mailbox. It's coming. Personalized notes are the future for businesses to have a trustworthy relationship.

Key Number Nine: Communication

This should be a two-way street with communication fluid—both from you, as their manager, and them, as direct reports. How often does miscommunication occur? You would be surprised how infectious this can be in the workplace. A structured system must be in place and prioritized. For example, let's suppose I'm a manager in a busy call center. My primary methods of communication are the following:

- Chat
- Phone
- Walk ups

If I was on a chat session with someone, and another agent walked up with a question, how do you prioritize who is first? Do you continue the chat sessions because you interacted with them first? Or do you help the person who's staring at you?

Let's turn it around: I'm an individual contributor in a busy call center. I'm on the phone with a customer, and another agent is standing behind me with a question. Who comes first? Do you ignore the agent or multi-task? These are all real things that happen and we must develop a system that works for your department.

These types of things should be seen and identified by you, as the manager, along with a plan of action in case these events occur. Whatever these instances are, we must identify them and give our teams the correct decision factors for each.

Key Number Ten: The Element of Surprise

Especially in fast paced environments, your days can be over in the blink of an eye and can be very redundant day in and day out. We, as managers, must develop a system that is constantly changing. We shouldn't be doing the same routine which the employees will be expecting. We need to invoke the element of surprise and do things differently to allow that winning spirit to shine among your agents. When your team is not expecting a change, we are catching them with the element of surprise. Even if it's something small like mixing up the team's desks and changing their environment, it goes a long way.

By doing the items in Chapter Four: "What Defines Me?" and in Chapter Six: "The Element of Surprise," you will keep your team guessing every day.

36. Blending Management Styles Without a Blender

In my opinion, there are four different management styles. I have identified them below. A good leader will need to blend and use all of these styles, rather than just one, in order to succeed.

Style # 1: Factual

This leader is providing change and coaching by using factual data to support their decision. This type of style focuses on:

- The 'factual' manager by showing the data
- Helps show change by using charts of factual data
- Helps drive performance by sharing where they are, where they are going, and where they are now.

This leader may use techniques such as: Erlang C for proper forecasting of occupancy. Erlang C is a traffic modeling formula used in call center scheduling to calculate delays or predict waiting times for callers. Erlang C bases its formula on three factors: the number of reps providing service, the number of callers waiting, and the average amount of time it takes to serve each caller.

Example of using an Erlang C calculator to determine agents needed:

Calculate the number of agents required to reach an agreed service level:

Incoming call rate	25	calls per half hour
Average call duration	360	seconds
Required service level	99.0%	
Probability of target answer time		
Target answer time	60	seconds
Number of Agents requir	**11**	

This same manager will not shy away from running an ad-hoc report to determine data on many factors, such as (but not limited to):

- CPAH (Calls Per Available Hour)
- Talk Time (With and Without Hold)
- AUX Modes
- Attendance Tracking (Login – Logout)
- Tracking of Lunch or Breaks
- Talk time per skill or line of business
- Occupancy

Style # 2: Coacher

This style has the primary objective of the employees' professional success:

- The 'developmental' manager for shaping the employee.
- Shows their weaknesses and strengths.
- Captain for professional development.

This manager knows the importance of coaching the advisor in real time by spot checking their work. They often have conversations surrounding training and different advice on soft skills and the quality of work. This manager is interested in the job growth of their employees, and provides the coaching and training they need.

Style # 3: Cheerleaders

This style has the primary objective of the direct staff being part of the changes that are put into place. They are allowed to submit initiative changes and are rewarded for their efforts

- The 'team oriented' manager for the "we're in this together" tone of mind.
- Encourages employees to come up with answers as a team.
- Rewards the team.

This manager is not alone and wants the team to know they are part of the bigger picture. Being the front line staff, they are also in charge of making the department better.

Style # 4: Visionary

- The visionary style has the primary objective of providing direction and clear vision for the team.
- The 'orchestra' manager has the timing vision of where the team is going
- Known to provide clear direction along with expectations.

- This manager is interested in setting a consistent pace every day.

This manager has done the agent's role before and has a clear vision of where the staff needs to go and how they are going to get there. Much like an orchestra, the timing and consistency is something that needs to be on pace every day.

When you're managing, your teams think about these styles. Ask yourself one question: am I all of these, or just one? If you're only one-sided, then you need to start putting these other qualities inside that one specific quality and blend them together to successfully lead. We cannot lead in black and white. We must have some color and must blend these four types of management styles together.

37. Misdirection

Think about this date for a minute: December 25th. On this date, especially with children, it's a hectic month leading up to December 25th, which, of course is formally known now as 'Christmas'; or more traditionally, "The Birth of Christ." In my house, it's a busy time of the year. But the gift of having your children's hopes and dreams become unwrapped by living that moment of happiness sure is rewarding. This is the time of the year where we, as parents, implement 'Misdirection.' My definition of 'misdirection' is as follows:
[mis-di-rek-shuh-n]
'What the eyes see and the ears hear, the mind believes.'

We, as parents, implement misdirection every year when it's time to prep for Santa. This type of illusion typically does not last long, but we are good in selling the white lies to make the time of year more memorable.

If you have ever seen movies such as: "*Knight and Day*," they use this tactic of misdirection to illustrate a moment that doesn't have any logic; and sometimes, you overlook it and correct it in your mind. On one particular moment in this movie, during a bank robbery, the writers created a line that I bet not everyone noticed. With a gun drawn to a head of a hostage, the character says, "I'm going to kill myself and then, I'm going to kill her." Did I hear that right?

I'm going to challenge you to put this to the test and think of a scenario that makes no logical sense, and state it during a formal or informal meeting. Will anyone catch it? If not, did we correct this logic automatically in our mind, and simply ignored the fact that the statement is impossible? Now, those who do question it are logical, active listeners who probably do very well in gathering and repeating scenarios back to customers.

Origin of Traffic Lights

Have you ever wondered why traffic lights are the color they are today? This color scheme derives from a system used by the railroad industry since the 1830s. At the time, railroad companies developed a means of letting train engineers know when to stop or go, using different colored lights representing different actions.

They chose red as the color for stop. It is thought, for centuries that red is associated with danger. For the other colors, they chose white as the color for go, and green as the color for caution.

The choice of a white light for go turned out to cause a lot of problems; such as an incident in 1914 where a red lens fell out of its holder and left the white light behind it got exposed. This ended with a train running a 'stop' signal and crashing into another train. Thus, the railroad decided to change it, so that the green light meant go and the yellow was used for caution; primarily because the color is so distinct from the other two used.

Based on these facts, you can see how the way things are has been based on historical use, and how they change over time based on those experiences. This is much the same in the workplace, when we implement a change and make minor tweaks to it, so that it's even better than it was.

Origin of God's Vision of Men

Perception of one's idea is based on your observations, which could lead your mind into misdirection. For example: do you believe God is a sexist? Let me explain why I say this.

Think about this for a minute: is this the perception we have all had engraved onto our minds? When we watch movies, this common line is often said, "For all of <u>man</u>kind, as you know it." Notice that I have underlined the word 'man'.

For many years, the typical construction worker on the highway would be putting up signs that said: "Men Working." As you will notice, both the words used to describe worker's working on a highway and the way movies describe the world are the same. They are using the words that reference men or man in these sentences.

It's December and in Connecticut, we sure get our fair amount of snow, and of course, our children love outside activities in the snow. When they want to build something out of snow, what do they call it? They sure don't say snow person, they say "I want to build a snowman." Again, the word 'man' is embedded into our minds, as we have phrased this type of action over many years.

As time has moved on, our perception of what a person is capable of is most certainly changing. Women are now doing the same type of work, as men; God's initial vision probably was for men to be branded to do certain things. With those thoughts in mind, our brain has engraved these things to be done by men only.

Illustration of Origin of God's Vision of Men

However, we, as a society, have changed the initial vision God has created for us, and have allowed women to be more inclusive with their branding in the workforce.

During this day and age, women are not just staying at home and playing the typical role as 'housewife/mom'. They are doing much more. Times have changed and so should our impression of the word 'women' and what that means to us.

Next, I'm going to hit on a very opinionated topic, which has also changed from what God's initial vision was. I'm referring to God's vision of man and woman, now becoming man and man, or woman and woman. As our society is adapting to these types of relationships as acceptable, and with many states allowing same sex marriage, we most certainly have changed God's initial vision of what is acceptable and understood.

Think about your workplace in the perception of what your team may believe in. How did they arrive to that conclusion? Just because that's how it has been, doesn't mean the perception or the end result cannot be changed. It can; point in case with this example.

Our society is adapting for the need to change based on what's accepted in our environment.

We need to ensure our workforce understands this concept. We need to also emphasize the point: that not changing can be a rocky road to disaster, and really upsell the importance of change, adapting to our environments, and the needs of the workplace.

The Supernatural Are Among Us

This is a good exercise to do with your team to emphasize the point of: "you don't need to see something to believe in it." How many times are you presented with an issue that you may not have all of the pieces in front of you to firmly connect the pieces. For example: boldly ask your team, "Do you believe in ghosts?" Go around the room and for those who say "yes"; ask them if they have seen any ghosts before. You will find that the majority who do believe in ghosts have not even seen one. Next, continue to ask them why they believe in them if they have not seen one before.

Think about things you are faced with during your everyday work cycle. Just because you have not seen it, before doesn't mean you don't believe in it.

Many of us believe in ghosts, but have not yet seen any. Just because we believe in something, does not mean it's something we have seen before. Just like in a call center, if you don't have the product, but have the general understanding of the product, then you should be able to build confidence and troubleshoot this model.

38. Manage, Don't Threaten

How many times do you remember in having a heated discussion with your children? Perhaps a situation where they wanted something right now, but you had to explain to them why they could not get it. My daughter often speaks about getting her own tablet device. We need to let them earn the device through good practice and not let our emotions get the better of us during heated discussions. For example: during Christmas time, in December 2005, we were shopping at Target. In the aisle behind us, I heard a conversation go like this:

"You put that back now, or Christmas is over. You won't be getting a single present and I'm telling Santa to put you on the naughty list."

How do you think that child felt? She probably felt demoralized by the words from her mother that day. The fact is: there are better ways to manage the situation than to use evil threats.

During 2006, I ran into a situation much like this when I was an individual contributor. I had just recently been converted from a contractor and into a full-time employee. A week later, a co-worker of mine had also received an employee offer that he wanted to discuss with me. As an individual contributor at the time, I didn't know that sharing offer information was something that would get me in trouble, or that he would mention my name during a hiring conversation. He had asked me what I was offered and then told me what he was offered. I told him he could squeeze another grand out of the offer and that he should counter.

During that employee's hiring conversation, he mentioned my name and said, "Joe received X amount and that's why I am countering." They eventually agreed on an amount and he was hired into the department.

The very next day, the manager called me into the office and asked, "Why are you sharing salary information?" They said that I could be replaced in the blink of an eye and that there are hundreds of people like me that could be found very easily.

"Knock it off, or you will be replaced by someone off the street."

Now, of course what I did was wrong, but I was not expecting the employee to mention my name during that conversation. After the discussion with the manager and being threatened, how do you think I felt?

This news was very demoralizing to me, and my impression of the manager was that they ran this department by demoralizing employees with threats. My purpose as an agent did not matter and they did not care about what my purpose was there at that position.

Of course, after due time with the same company, I proved them wrong and showed them that I'm not just anyone off the street—that I had value and proved myself along the way by being promoted. Threats are not the right way to manage an employee.

A good manager would have handled this situation differently and would not use threats as their main response. A good manager would have explained how offers are generated and what they look for in their decision to make an offer; for things such things: as education, related years of experience, certifications, and so on. My interactions with this manager relayed on threats with emotion to demoralize the staff.

Moving forward, now, as a manager, it's very important when you discuss promotions or offers with the employee, so that they know this information is for their eyes only. This story is a good example of the danger of sharing certain information with others.

39. Proper Design

If you have children, then you know the joys of a long road trip. It can be very challenging. For example: when we took a trip to Tennessee, my daughter would constantly try to change the radio. While we were stopped at a parking lot, she would lunge over and try to hit the 'scan' button on the vehicle's dashboard. What's interesting is that on my vehicle in particular, she asked why the button was all the way to the right. She said it was easy for her to change the channel, but looked far away for me to hit the button. She was absolutely right. It starts with a proper design.

This next lesson will focus on the proper design; which is the key for employee success.

Let's focus on the above panel for a moment and talk about a good design versus a bad design. When traveling on the road, there is one button that should be at eye level and on the driver's side, even if it isn't often needed or used. I'm referring to the emergency hazard button. In the above picture, look at where the emergency hazard button is. It's closer for the passenger to push it as opposed to the driver.

Also, in the above image, some other buttons seem to be less important and also towards the passenger seat. These buttons are the 'scan' and 'CD track change' buttons.

Would you consider this a convenient design? Or more importantly: a safe design—if I needed to put on my emergency lights? The answer is 'no.'

Let's keep the proper design concept in mind for a moment with your respective teams. It all starts with the employee and how they operate for their daily workflow. In order to ensure a proper design, it's up to you to ensure they have the necessary workflow in order.

When sitting with the employee, look at the following factors (if this is a call center agent):

1. As the call is incoming to their line, what are they doing to prepare for the call? What I mean by that is: what windows are open on what screens, and how are they navigating screens and using resources?
2. Are they multi-tasking and typing information—whether in raw notes or into the template—while it's being given to them?
3. How is their organization of their real estate (computer)? Do they have proper filing for important documents, whether they are on the computer or in their desk?
4. Are they utilizing proper keyboard or window shortcuts to save time?

By sitting with support staff, maybe website support, look at the following factors:

1. When developing a website, is the design easy and accessible?
2. If you can't find something, then it has a failed design.

3. Is the Proper Help or Contact Page easy to find?
4. Is the proper search easy to find?

You will notice variations from employee to employee, and by sitting with your staff, it's important to understand their design and how they apply their design every day.

This will be a great opportunity to find employees who have no design and are not consistent in their resources and navigation of the call. These employees will need to apply a proper design, so that they have a rhythm and purpose for each call.

40. Navigating Obstacles Together

The fall seems to be a favorite time for children, because of: hay rides, corn fields, and apple cider. My daughter and son enjoyed a puzzle of navigating a corn field. Together, we would work to find the proper exit to get out of the corn maze. The key is working together to find a solution. Your staff should feel involved and operate in the same way: solving obstacles together.

A few things that can spark some great group conversation in your team can be done by involving them in your department's challenges. Here is what you need for this exercise of solving problems as a team:

- A whiteboard or easel with paper

- A topic
- Your team, of course

Problem One: Think Of One Thing You Need To Be More Productive At As an Individual Contributor

During an informal meeting, let the team know that tomorrow, you need their help with this topic. Let them know to think of their idea and bring it with them tomorrow to discuss it with the team.

How It Works

✓ Each employee will write their idea on the whiteboard, and then their name next to the idea.

✓ The employee will then explain their idea and how it can help them become more productive

And Then....The Element of Surprise

As you learned in Chapter Six, the element of surprise is needed in the workplace. This exercise is no different. One of the things the staff doesn't know is: depending on the topic, I start using others as their mentor. Their mentor will help put a plan together to help them overcome the challenge, so that they are more productive.

What you will notice is that employees will start working together to solve problems. This type of team chemistry is needed in your environment, and this is the perfect vehicle to bring up the chemistry in your team.

If you look at what we just championed, these are the following results:

✓ Individual issues become a team issue.

✓ Team now makes an effort in solving an individual problem by being their mentor.

✓ Manager may also be a mentor as needed.

✓ This philosophy is applied to all employees.

What's Next?

✓ Carve time for the employee and mentor to propose their idea, to make them more productive.

✓ Manager will provide a deadline.

✓ Manager will implement this change pending budget.

✓ Manager will track their idea, project, and time management, and will make note during the performance review. Did they succeed?

41. Catching Fish Without a Fishing Pole

One of the things that my daughter saw while I was flipping the channels was a few guys in a boat in the middle of the lake. They were fishing for bass fish and my daughter was interested in seeing some fish. However, as we left the T.V. on for a few minutes, she asked, "What's the point?" I told her that this requires patience and timing to find the right spot for the fish.

Think about it: when you go fishing, most people will bring some beverages, or perhaps a cooler of beer. What occurs is in most cases, you may catch some fish, but are you fishing or are you drinking in a boat? Wouldn't it be interesting if you made it to the middle of the lake and you kicked up your feet on the cooler, and fish just magically jumped into your boat?

As this happens, keep in mind that you put in no effort other than getting out to the middle of the lake. This leads into automation in your departments; so, minimum effort is put on your staff and you, as their manager.

Phone IVR Automation

Let's look at the very basic concept of what information we are collecting while the call comes in. Are you capturing such information, so that it saves time on the agent's end?

✓ Asset Tag or Serial Number
✓ Customer Name and Contact Information

✓   Customer Location

By acquiring this simple information, we are saving time for the agents, because they don't have to ask for this information.

IVR Technology: Are You Using It?

Are you using everything possible from your technology to enhance the convenience you provide to your customers?

For example: most IVRs will allow you to setup assistance for the following items:

1. Password resets with security verification.
2. Allow you to save your spot and get a call back.
3. Check status of tickets with automated phone agent to provide you information.

These are just a few examples of the power you are able to setup for your phone tree. Take advantage of all of these options.

Technology Is Among Us

How many of us enjoy the traffic we are faced with while traveling to the office every day? I know this is my least favorite moment of the day, and quite frankly, a waste of time. Not to mention it's not enjoyable or relaxing anymore; it comes with stress.

Car ownership in China is rising, with an estimated 20 million new drivers occupying space on the road. In China, they are considering options for a way to carry a thousand passengers from one point to another, without taking up any space on the road.

The bus would span two traffic lanes and will most certainly allow fluid travel even in traffic jams, since it passes over vehicles. It would travel up to 40 miles an hour above street level on a special track, allowing regular cars fewer than seven feet high to freely pass underneath.

More importantly, it would run on electricity and take the place of 40 buses, which could cut annual fuel consumption by 800 tons and carbon emissions by almost 2,500 tons per the engineer in charge of the design. Whether this takes off or not, it's most certainly a great plan that could solve traffic congestion, and it can provide a relaxing ride as well.

Changing Lanes

How often on the highway do you see drivers shifting in and out of lanes? Does anybody know the reason for this? Is it because they are speeding and are a bad driver? Or is it simply because the left lane is being occupied by drivers going slower than the speed limit? It's a very opinionated topic.

Think about your organization and how often you have to 'change lanes' in a call center, in order to get that call to someone. Where is the automation in play? One must look at the bigger picture, which starts with the following factors:

1. Know your business.
2. Run reports on incoming calls by skill or product.
3. By doing so, do you have the right amount or agents to handle the load?

If we are constantly changing lanes and shifting people to take different calls, this is a clear indication that your center is not as automated as it should be. What do I mean by that? As a manager, you should be confident that you are able to sit back and let your agents answer the calls they are skilled for. There should be no interaction from you to start changing lanes.

By having the right automation in place, this will free you up to do other things, such as (but not limited to):

1. Sitting with your folks and coaching them in real time.
2. Working with the strategic manager to tighten up policies and procedures to ensure the center is running at optimum levels.
3. Developing your staff to be ready for their goals and mutually commit to those goals.
4. By sitting with your folks, identify training gaps in real time and plan accordingly.

42. Secret Ingredients for Success

During my career, I feel that my success has been based on many factors during my sixteen years in the industry. I have been successful in my career; first starting as an individual contributor because, quite simply, I had a vision of what needed to be done and I executed that vision. Let's take a quick look at some secret ingredients that should help you throughout your career.

Ingredient One: Understand the Job and Beat the Snot Out Of It

In 2006, I was looking for a challenge and more of a corporate type of job that could see my potential. I worked with a recruiter who mentioned a position that was 100% phone support with technical ability. At that time, I told the recruiter that the technical part was not an issue, but that I had never done phone support before. They said, "We understand. I think you would be great for the job" and then submitted my resume. When the hiring manager got my resume, they saw the recruiter had mentioned that I had phone experience on my resume. I had to explain the little phone experience I had, but I was eager to prove myself. I did get a phone call the next week and landed the job, so I was very excited that the recruiter company had stretched the truth about my background.

Within in a month of getting the position, I hit the ground running and knew the call center in and out. I wanted to be number one, so that the management team would understand my value. I carefully, within the next week, performed the following consistently:

- Took over 100 calls.
- Had less repeat callers with a true FCR (first call rating).
- Trusted source of information (almost veteran of knowledge after 2 months).
- Performance sheets handed to me with # 1 each week.
- Got quickly promoted.

Remember: that the key to success when working with other individual contributors is to stand out from the crowd. I did just that for my management team to recognize my talent. This goes back to Chapter 9 regarding the 'McGee Success Ladder'; by understanding the role and then beating the snot out of it.

Ingredient Two: Do More

This is a very simple concept to understand and means exactly what it says. Think about your organization and how many leaders there are in your department right now. How do you think you rank against your subordinates?

My key to success started in 2009, with simply doing more. It is the key for your value to be seen by your direct boss. We must involve ourselves in projects and keep busy—but more importantly: we must take initiative to take on new initiatives and own them. When it comes time to compare you to your other managers, it's going to come down to what their value is. What kind of projects and initiatives did you own and execute? The next time you are writing your weekly report to your boss, pay attention to the small or big list of accomplishments, and quite determine whether they are possibly bigger than your subordinates. The key is to do your current job and stay busy, and do more—which is sounds very easy but requires patience, organization, and prioritization of tasks.

The worst-case scenario everyone needs to instill in their mind is: the possibility of RIFs (Reduction in Force) across all business segments. When your boss starts to look at your accomplishments and you are doing the bare minimum, do you think you are safe? Think again. By staying busy, you are securing your job. This type of understanding for me started in 2009, has continued stuck to my mindset for many years, and it is how I am able to stay successful.

Ingredient Three: Always Be One Step Ahead

There will be a time in your career, it may not be tomorrow or in the next 10 years, but it will come. This day when you're shut out of what may be occurring in your department. Perhaps, you start to be shut out of meetings and are kept in the dark about the future of your department. When this day comes—and it will come—you need a contingency plan to protect your future. I want you to think about a fighter, whether it's a boxer or someone who practices mixed martial arts, and think about their weaknesses. Many opponents often will watch prior recordings to think of a way to overcome their weakness and ultimately win the match. In sports, this is no different. Many coaches and individual players will do this to get the edge for their next match.

This same type of thinking applies to your workplace. There will always be a soft spot in which it's vulnerable to be, let's say, 'exposed.'

I won't go into further detail about how to find out information that was not intended for you, but a smart leader will find the vulnerabilities; and by doing so, you will find the information to make an informed decision about their future. This type of thinking has helped me be one step ahead of my seniors earlier in my career.

This type of risk was needed to determine my future outcome. Now, of course, my practices taken in order to find the truth were not ideal, but were worth the risk. In management, you always need to balance your decisions and weigh the risk and reward. For me, this risk was worth the reward; which allowed me to make a decision to move onto another position. If you want to know more specifically about this experience, attend my boot camp courses available for more insight.

Ingredient Four: Equal Playing Field and Everyone Needs To See That

Often times, managers will make the mistake of showing favoritism to one particular direct report. Maybe, they are friends. Maybe, this person works from home more than others, or is involved in special projects. Believe it or not, this is a recipe for disaster. Think about your perception as their manager and this is exactly how rumors will start if favoritism is there.

A good manager should run their operation just like a business: on an equal playing field. As part of my success story, it's crucial to run your operation as a business and not a friendship. If you're new to management, this is something you must know not to do.

43. The Darkest Hour

During my career, I feel that my success is based on many factors, including experiencing the darkest hour; which is the darkest time in your life.

In this book, this last chapter will reinforce how my children were almost not born, and how this book would not have been written. For me, the darkest hour started on July 28, 2006, in which the happiest day of my life turned into the darkest hour of my life. I wanted to share this very personal moment in my life to illustrate that being defeated is not the answer.

This last chapter is a reminder of God's blessing and in retrospect, how things can change by finding out all the facts and arriving at a solution.

Things were moving forward, and I was about to become a father for the first time. But that all changed on July 28, 2006. My wife was at the hospital and was only three or four months pregnant. In that moment, everything was about to be taken away from me. The doctor informed me that there was nothing he could do, and that I had lost my child. This moment was hard for me to accept, as I was in a panic, and my heart was beating out of my chest. Moments later, I fainted and found myself waking up on the floor being revived with Epsom salt by several nurses.

When I awoke, I found that my first child had died; and I saw him for the first time. He was so beautiful and somewhat defined. I saw his little hair, fingers, feet, and toes. But that was gone in a blink of an eye. This pain is something that is indescribable and something that was very hard for me to accept. Having a miscarriage and thinking you would never have children was a splinter in my mind I could not escape.

Now, ten years later, I remember words that my wife's grandmother, Eleanor, said during my son's funeral. On that day of mourning, she said, "It's going to be okay. You are going to have lots of children." Eleanor has always been the kind of person to instill reassurance and hope in unfavorable conditions. Even though these words resonated with me for so many years, in that moment, I knew there was a rocky road in store for me. I looked at my wife and knew that I would never have children, and that I was about to disappoint myself and my wife with that in-ability to have children. A tear emerged in my eye and I started to bite my lip, knowing that our dream of children was not in the cards.

This ate at me for several days, months, and ultimately, years; knowing I had to accept defeat.

A turning point in 2009 came, when we discovered that my wife could have an operation called a 'cerclage.' There was a chance it could give us the ability to do something we didn't think was possible anymore: have children.

Cerclage is the use of a ring or loop to bind together the ends of an obliquely fractured bone, or to encircle the opening of a malfunctioning cervix.

In 2009, when my wife was pregnant, I was very unsure if I would relive my darkest hour once again, and for the entire year, I was very sad and uncertain about what was going to happen. For many who know me personally, I have a strong poker face in the workplace and don't show my emotions or bring the challenges of my personal life into the workplace.

The 'cerclage' typically cannot be performed until four months into the pregnancy, which was very scary, since that was the same time when we lost our first child. When we made it to the doctors for her to get the operation, it was discovered she was eight-centimeters dilated, and we were on the verge of losing our child, again. As the doctor informed me of this news, my mind was racing at a million frames per second. I was a train wreck and did not want to hear the news for the second time. He ensured me that he was going to do everything he could. Time passed, and the doctor emerged. I was shaking and was a mess waiting for the news on the operation. He told me everything was fine and my wife and baby were safe. She was a miracle baby in the making, and we were so thrilled that things were looking up.

In August 2009, the doctor had given us the date to come back and have the cerclage removed and ultimately, we were going to have the baby sometime between August 25 and August 26. On August 25, something amazing happened: the birth of Ursula McGee, who came into this world and was most certainly a miracle baby. We were so thrilled to have defeated our darkest hour, and we were now living in the happiest days of our lives.

However, things did begin to turn the other way during the night Ursula was sleeping with us in the hospital. That night, she turned purple and was rushed into the Intensive Care Unit. She went in for a checkup and was in the ICU for a period of several weeks. After a few weeks, thankfully, she made a full recovery and is a true miracle baby.

Moving forward with our other children, we knew that we could not have them the traditional way with the other two; a 'cerclage' was needed. But we have accepted that is how we must have children, and it did, in fact, work for us.

If you are a new manager or a current manager, you will soon realize that you will face many challenges and dark times throughout your career, or in your personal life. Be patient. Answers will find the way to turn these dark sides into blessed moments.

Eleanor, my wife's grandmother had passed away in October of 2016, and I know she is very happy that we did, in fact, have lots of children just like her initial vision of what was expected.

Usrula means 'little bear.' It is derived from a diminutive form of the Latin word *ursa* or 'she-bear.' Saint Ursula was a legendary virgin princess of the 4th century, who was martyred by the Huns while returning from a pilgrimage. In England, the saint was popular during the middle ages, and the name came into general use at that time.

As you can see with this closing chapter, my daughter has come a long way to get into this world. This book is dedicated to my daughter, Ursula Morgana McGee, for having the strength and courage to come into this world.

MCGEE ⚡ LEADERSHIP

Joseph McGee is expanding his teachings through this book into an exciting bootcamp format with classes in Connecticut. If you would like Joseph McGee to come to your location, it can be arranged through his website.

For a class schedule and price of the bootcamp classes, or if you would like to engage with Joseph McGee in a private speaking event or a bootcamp at your location, visit his website at: http://mcgeeleadership.com

Stay connected with the author by following them on the following social media pages:

Twitter: @Scorpionkingct
Facebook: http://facebook.com/mcgeeleadership

Email: jmcgee@mcgeeleadership.com
YouTube:
https://www.youtube.com/user/ScorpionKingInCT

New Exercises

Misdirection in the Technical World
   [mis-di-rek-shuh-n]
   'What the eyes see and the ears hear, the mind believes.'

   In this exercise, we are using the techniques from Chapter 5: "Show and Tell Is a Must," in which objects are used to enhance points.

   Let's look at the above object. What do you see from afar?
   It appears to be money, and does look much like a $20 Dollar Bill.

Applying this exercise at the workplace in a few easy steps:

Step 1: Show this item to your team from 10-15 feet away and ask them what this item is. Your team will most likely say "money" or "a $20-dollar bill."

Step 2: Start to move closer to your team (Walk towards them).

Step 3: Ask them to look closer and ask them what they see. Is this money?

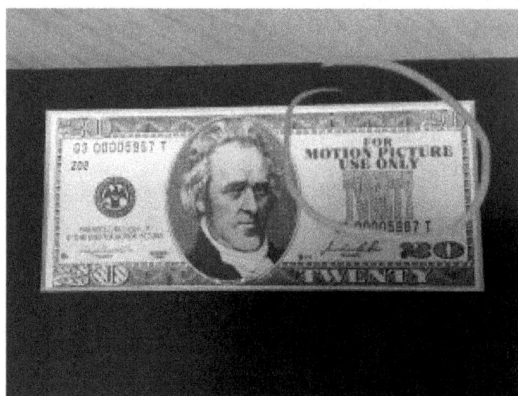

Selling Points for the Exercise:

1. Tell your team that much like in technical troubleshooting, when we are the receiver sometimes, the information being circulated to us may not be all the facts. It's not until we get closer or get our eyes focused the issue is when we get a clearer picture of the true issue. How many times do you work an issue and notice that either all the facts given were wrong or missing? Therefore, we must be the bridge and have our eyes on the issue, so that the facts are not missed. Look at this exercise from afar; we thought this was money. When we got closer, we learned that this is: 'Motion Picture ONLY prop money.' This is not real money. We only came to that conclusion by taking a closer look.

Let me ask you: are you taking the time to get a closer look? Are you performing remote sessions to get all eyes on the issue? Are you asking for videos or screenshots? It's not that trust is lost after what they say, it's that second eyes are ALWAYS needed.

Did you see it?

Not all eyes will have noticed this next part from this exercise...Did you notice it?

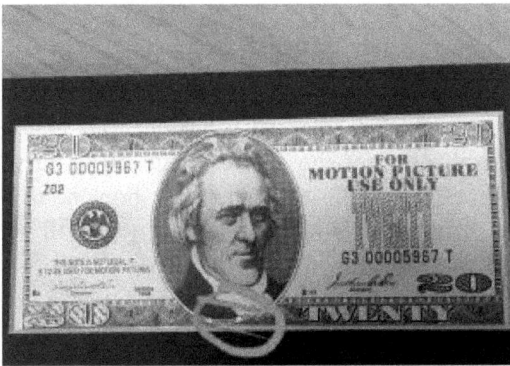

Who is supposed to be on the $20 dollar bill? Andrew Jackson.

Therefore, a second set of eyes is crucial for success.

What's the Answer?

$$\text{🍌} + \text{🍌} = 30$$

$$\text{🍒🍒} + \text{🍒🍒} = 20$$

$$\text{🍎} + \text{🍎} = 8$$

$$\text{🍌} + \text{🍒} \times \text{🍎} = ?$$

Do you know the answer? What if I told you that each person could interpret the above riddle differently? If you were to give this riddle to your team, how many answers would be different? I will tell you that you will see varied answers.

Conclusion

In the technical world, we must NOT overlook taking a closer look. Always have another eye on the issue to confirm all the facts before assuming and working deep into an issue. I hope this will spark some ideas in your workplace with your teams.

Prop Money

Where do I find Prop Money? You can find Prop money on eBay.

New Exercises
Go to the Olympics

What do we know about the Olympics? We know that it is very competitive. Bring your team to the Olympics using objects and storytelling.

The modern 'Olympic Games' or 'the Olympics' are a leading international sporting events featuring summer and winter sports competitions in which thousands of athletes from around the world participate in a variety of competitions. The Olympic Games are considered the world's foremost sports competition. The Olympic Games are held every four years, with the Summer and Winter Games alternating by occurring every four years, but they are two years apart.

Their creation was inspired by the ancient Olympic Games, which were held in Olympia, Greece, from the 8th century BC to the 4th century AD. All these athletes want the gold medals and have trained for this event, representing over 200 nations.

What will you need for this exercise?

Three Medals: gold, bronze, and silver that you will hand to your team.

Conceptional design of exercise

You will need (3) volunteers for this exercise and (1) judge.

Step 1: Give it a name

Call it the (Your Department Name) Olympics; Soaring Paper Airplane Challenge. Play Olympic Music while you are explaining the rules.

Step 2: Rules

Rules. Make a starting 'throwing line' and designate a paper basket for the target. Each competitor will have 5 minutes to make the best airplane. Each competitor will throw only one airplane. The judge will color mark each airplane, so that there is no confusion as to who threw what plane. The competitor closest to the target deemed by the judge is the winner.

Step 3: Award Medal

Provide the medals for 1st, 2nd, and 3rd place winners. They will keep the medals

Step 4: Purpose

Explain to them after the demonstration, that everyone here today wanted the gold medal. We strive as athletes in the Olympics to be the best; 100% of the time.

The Connection >>

This is just like our internal surveys that we receive. We want to be the best and reduce the poor—or very poor—feedback. Please remember that in this demonstration, we must give 100% of our the time to our customers.

Conclusion

This exercise was used to bridge the connection between surveys, the drive, and the determination of each person wanting that 'gold medal.' Use this exercise to bring that connection to your team, or perhaps think of one like this that relates to your department. Making that proper connection is crucial in understanding the importance of department goals.

www.ingramcontent.com/pod-product-compliance
Lightning Source LLC
Chambersburg PA
CBHW060025210326
41520CB00009B/1008